The Towpath

Arch Merrill's New York

A River Ramble
The Lakes Country
The Ridge
The Towpath
Rochester Sketch Book
Stagecoach Towns
Tomahawks and Old Lace
Land of the Senecas
Upstate Echoes
Slim Fingers Beckon
Shadows on the Wall
Southern Tier – Volume I
Southern Tier – Volume II
The White Woman and Her Valley
Our Goodly Heritage
Pioneer Profiles
Bloomers and Bugles
Gaslights and Gingerbread
Fame in Our Time
Down the Lore Lanes
The Underground
The Changing Years
From Pumpkin Hook to Dumpling Hill

The Towpath

by
Arch Merrill

Fourth of a Series

Empire State Books
Interlaken, New York

Library of Congress Cataloging-in-Publication Data

Merrill, Arch.
  The Towpath.

  (Arch Merrill's New York)
  Reprint. Orginally published: New York: A. Merrill, 1945.
  "Fourth of a series"
  1. Erie Canal Region (N.Y.)—History, Local. 2. Erie Canal
Region (N.Y.)—Social life and customs. I. Title. II. Series:
Merrill, Arch. New York.
  F127.E5M47 1989   974.7—dc19   88-2636—CIP
  ISBN: 1-55787-001-2 (pbk.)

First published by the author in 1945
Reprinted by Creek Books
Reprinted by Empire State Books
September 1989 — 3000 copies.

ISBN: 1-55787-001-2
Manufactured in the United States

A *quality* publication of
Heart of the Lakes Publishing
Interlaken, New York 14847

*To the dwindling little band of men
who in a bygone day
"navigated on the Erie Canal"
And to all the friendly people
along the old Towpath who
were so kind to me, this
book is dedicated.*

Arch Merrill

The Author as a Tugboat Traveler

*"Low bridge, ev'rybody down!
Low bridge, for we're going through a town,
And you'll always know your neighbor,
You'll always know your pal,
If you've ever navigated on the Erie Canal."*

Tugboat Log

WELL, I "navigated" on the Erie Canal—for 14 hours.

But I don't think I was cut out for a canaller. For one thing, it means getting up too early.

The hands of the clock in the canal guard gate house, just west of the Genesee, pointed to 6:30, when I boarded the steam tug, Matton 21, on the raw morning of May 28 in the year of our Lord, 1945, and of the Erie Canal, 120.

To me, 6:30 a. m. is an hour that just does not exist. Ordinarily I get home from my stint at the newspaper office at 3:30 a. m. High noon is my usual hour for arising.

So it was a sleepy-eyed seeker after lore of the Towpath who scrambled awkwardly aboard the gasoline barge that the Matton 21 was pushing through Erie water from Utica to Tonawanda. After being a landlubber for two score years and ten, one does not start even 14 hours "before the mast" with marked agility or grace.

Of course, in following the Towpath from Medina to Clyde —the territory covered in this ramble—the ideal conveyance would have been a sleek packet boat with its hull painted a gleaming white and window blinds a rich green; a packet boat hauled by two horses trotting tandem with a driver astride the rear animal; a packet boat whose approach was heralded by the blast of a bugle and the strident cry of "Low bridge, everybody down!"

I might as well have wished for Cinderella's coach or Ben Hur's chariot. The hands of the clock can't be turned back a century. This was 1945 and not the packet days of 1845. Besides, the Towpath itself is only a memory now.

So I "hitched" a ride on a steam tug plying the modernized and undramatic Barge Canal, sans the trappings and glamor of Packet-Towpath days.

* * * *

In case you're figuring on going out to the canal bank and hailing the next passing boat for a ride, I warn you it's not that easy. My ride was the result of considerable correspondence. I was armed with the proper credentials from Ralph Matton, secretary-treasurer of the Matton Line of Waterford, when I nearly fell on my face getting aboard the gas barge his tug was pushing.

It was through the good offices of Theodore J. (Ted) Zornow of the Zornow Coal Company of Pittsford that I kept track of the movements of the Matton 21. The tug takes on coal at the Zornow yards. The morning I boarded her she had just received a four-day supply, 24 tons. Zornow told the captain he was to have a Medina-bound passenger, a reporter, at the Rochester west guard gate. The captain waggishly told the crew it would be a woman reporter. That explained the keen disappointment on the faces of the tug crew when they saw their passenger.

The Matton 21, a staunch craft, was built in 1908. She has seen service in New York's busy harbor as well as many years on the more quiet stretches of the canal. I was told it was the only steam tug operating on the Barge Canal this year. The rest are Diesel-powered.

I had visioned a day of lolling on a sunny deck. But I had reckoned without the weather gods that decreed the coldest, wettest spring in a generation. The wind blew violently out of the west; there were intermittent showers of rain and constant showers of cinders from the Matton's stack. So this passenger spent most of his time in the pilot house chatting with the steersmen, with frequent visits to the galley where Tony, the cook, served coffee at all hours.

The tug was bucking a strong, wind-whipped current and believe it or not, there can be considerable current on the Ditch you think so placid. We were not able to maintain even the orthodox four miles an hour "speed."

* * * *

In all the canal books I've read, the boatmen were pictured as rough, profane, brawling characters. I found the crew of the Matton 21 nothing of the kind.

The captain, fortyish Thomas F. Van Allen of Troy, is a gentlemanly, self-possessed, capable mariner who for 24 years was pilot and captain of a boat on the Hudson River Night Line of blessed memory. He has been on the canal the past six years. In his Hudson Line days, he met all kinds of people, politicos, magnates, sportsmen—even newswriters. He particularly remembers an affable Canadian who spent part of one night on the Hudson chatting in his pilot house. That passenger's name was Mackenzie King. Captain Van Allen was at the wheel when the last night boat made the New York-Albany run.

The mate and co-pilot, Napoleon "Poley" Miner of Schuylerville, has been "boatin' it" for nearly half a century. He was virtually raised on the inland waterways. This graying, black-eyed, slender veteran of the canal told many a tale of the long ago, when he relieved the captain at the wheel.

There were two engineers and two firemen, one a fellow Rochesterian, husky Edward Strong of 284 Clinton Ave. S., a veteran of the canal and lakes service. Firing a steam tug is no weakling's job. There were two deck hands, one a mere lad of about 17, and the other, a quiet, brown-eyed older youth, who had been in the bloody siege of Guadalcanal and did not like to talk about it.

And there was Tony, the cook, who once had owned his own restaurant. Cheerfully he ladled out coffee all day. Canal men are inordinate coffee drinkers. They feed well, too. I had two tasty, substantial meals in the little galley. We had STEAK for dinner and there was plenty of butter. Remember this was May, 1945.

On the gasoline barge of 400,000 gallons capacity that we were pushing, empty, up the long and lockless level between Rochester and Lockport were two employes of a big oil company. They have their own cabin on the barge. Like the crew of the Matton 21, they work the six-hour shift that has been traditional for men, horses and mules on the canal ever since the Ditch was dug.

*　　*　　*　　*

It's a lonely life on Erie water. Not often does the crew touch the green shores that are so near.

The men look forward to occasional night stopovers in towns. That means a break in the monotony of the six-hour trick and the slow, steady haul across the state. It means bowling and movies and maybe a few beers. "But," the captain said, "there are no drunks on this boat." Most of his crew are family men, with a sense of their responsibilities. A longing for home and family possesses them.

The old days, when there was a fight at every lock and canallers were the roughest, toughest tribe in all the land, are gone as irrevocably as are the towpath and the mules those brawlers drove.

There was a brief halt at Spencerport where Tony and one of the deck hands went ashore for grub and the morning newspapers.

They know most of the canal towns from brief stopovers. They can spot each village from afar by the church steeples. The buildings beside the old waterway fascinate them and they speculate on the age of the weather-beaten structures. Some of them were built in De Witt Clinton's day.

And ruins of once busy warehouses leer at the passing boats from a few gone-to-seed towns beside the slow waters.

The animal life on the green shores holds much interest for the boatmen, too. They told about the deer that swam for half a mile ahead of the barge; of the swarm of bees that all but nestled on the pilot house; of the mink, woodchucks and muskrats they see along the banks. The day I rode the tug, we all exclaimed at the sight of a dozen pheasants, half of them cocks, in a field near Knowlesville. "Oh for a gun!" cried one of the younger men.

The boaters get to know people who live beside the lazy waters. Down near South Greece, after we had passed through the cheerless chasm that canal folk call "The Rochester Rock Cut," is a trim white house. The captain and "Poley" both told of the boy and girl who live there and who have waved at them for seven years. "We used to toss them magazines and the comics we saved for them."

But the day I traveled the Long Level, there was nobody waving from in front of the white house. "The kids have grown up. The girl's away at school and the boy's working," the captain said. "They were little things when we first knew them."

There were times when the steersmen pulled the whistle cord

and not for any bridge or guard gate. It was just a greeting to old friends on land, who have come to watch for the tug.

Steering a canal boat looks easy but it's an art. In the old days it was entirely up to the strong arms of the wheelsman. Now he merely touches the wheel and machinery does the rest. But he has to be ever on the alert. In passing through a guard gate where there is only four feet leeway on either side, a wrong motion might send a barge laden with half a million gallons of gasoline into an abutment.

Approaching a lift bridge calls for three distinct whistle blasts. The signal is a familiar one to dwellers along the canal. The bridge tender answers and slowly the bridge rises. But not so long ago, something went wrong with the electrical apparatus that controlled one of the lift bridges. The bridge just did not go up and the barge was drifting slowly down upon it. A crewman threw a rope over a snubbing post just in time.

That incident was passed off as part of the "day's work."

I found no traffic congestion on the Barge Canal in 1945. All the way from Rochester to Medina the Matton 21 met only two tows, both of them tugs pushing "gas" barges. They were the Annie L. Connors and the John J. Tucker.

By the way, I found out that the down-stream or eastbound boat always has the right of way, an old rule of the Ditch.

*   *   *   *

That Towpath is still discernible at many points, although grass has pretty well covered it. Farmers and utilities use it at places for a highway—of sorts.

Bank watchers walk it, looking for breaks or other untoward occurrences. Along the Long Level there are concrete posts every mile. Each contains a time clock that the bank patrolman rings, even as a night watchman making his rounds in an office building.

These men, mostly elderly employes who in their time served the state in other capacities, cover a 15-mile stretch daily.

Farmers who live along the canal are continually filing claims against the state for damage done their land by seepage or breaks in the rubble-enforced walls. Sometimes burrowing muskrats cause these breaks. The Court of Claims calendar is always full of these water damage cases. But the old waterway also does many a farmer a good turn. In times of severe drought, many farmers have hauled away canal water to save their thirsty stock and their parched crops.

* * * *

"Poley," handling the wheel with a dexterity born of long practice, pointed to a section of still visible Towpath near Hulberton. "When I was 7 years old I rode one of my dad's mules there," he said.

"My father owned canal boats and I was raised on one, you might say. When I was a little codger, my mother used to tie me with a harness, attached to a strong hook atop the cabin so she could go about her housework, knowing I would not fall into the water.

"Our boat had awnings and flower boxes. It was white with green trimmings. Many families lived on the boats the year around, tieing up in basins for the winter in colonies like trailer camps today.

"I've been a boatin' all my life. I owned my own boat and mules before steam and the big companies took over and the Barge was constructed. I've seen great days on the canal."

"Fights?" and "Poley" grinned widely. "Yeah, I've seen plenty of 'em. Canal men were he-men in hee-haw days."

They are gone now, those rough, picturesque days of the Towpath, the mules and the cursing, hard-drinking "hoggies" that drove them. Gone are the weighlocks, the cross-over bridges, the heel-path, the canal groceries and grog shops at every look, the battles over crossed tow lines and the battles just for the love of battle.

"Poley" Miner is of French-Canadian stock. His wife is dead. His two younger children live with his aged mother in Schuylerville and go to school there. His oldest boy, in the family tradition, is on a Navy tanker in the Pacific. "Poley" was hoping he'd get home over Memorial Day. "But you never know in this business," he commented.

He figures he'll have to retire soon. How he will miss the feel of the wheel and the six-hour trick and the sound of the water sloshing against the tug. For he's "been a boatin' " all his life.

What do tug men do in the winters after the waterway is closed? Well, many work on the tugs in the ice-free Eastern harbors.

It was 8:30 p.m. when the good ship Matton 21 wound through the serpentine curves that carry the canal through Medina Town.

The captain maneuvered the barge and tug up to the little used dock back of the rows of gray buildings, built of the enduring Medina sandstone, in the brisk, prosperous town that was born of the Clinton Ditch.

I jumped clumsily from the bow of the barge. Again I nearly fell. The crew waved and called: "Good-bye and good luck." I waved back. The Matton 21 steamed away.

I'll bet I was the first passenger to land at Medina's canal dock in many a moon.

As I walked up an alley into the main street, I heard three familiar whistle blasts. The tug was signaling for the lift bridge. I could visualize the captain's strong hands pulling at the cord. To me it was farewell to a good ship and a swell crew.

Later on, when I followed the Towpath in other and faster conveyances—all the way from the gorge of the Oak Orchard to the bonnie banks of the Clyde—I kept a lookout for the Matton 21. I saw the Annie L. Connors again at Lyons, and the Tucker at Fairport but never a glimpse of my tug.

But always, in the days to come whenever I hear the hoarse whistles calling from Erie water, I will remember My Day on the canal, my 14 hours on 47 miles of the Long Level, my first day of many along the old Towpath.

Ditch of Destiny

ONCE upon a time many years ago, there lived here in York State men who had a splendid dream.

They visioned a Grand Canal linking the waters of Lake Erie and the Hudson River that flows into the Atlantic.

They sought out Thomas Jefferson and the Sage of Montecello told them: "You are a century too soon."

But the dogged Yorkers did not choose to wait another hundred years. They went ahead and built the Erie Canal.

President Madison told them: "Your scheme would exhaust the resources of the nation."

So New York built her canal alone—without a penny of federal aid. In 10 years it had paid for itself.

Backwoods wiseacres scoffed: "You can't make boats run uphill." They lived to see canal boats floating (uphill) past their doors in a steady stream.

In 1812, Tammany Hall, blind in its hatred of DeWitt Clinton, derided his "Ditch" in vitriolic doggerel that wound up with the line: "Why grin? It will do to bury its mad author in."

Thirteen years later, on Oct. 26, 1825, the windows of Tammany Hall rattled to the booming of cannon. That salute, relayed by guns that lined the Towpath all the way from Buffalo to Sandy Hook, proclaimed that DeWitt Clinton, governor of New York, was riding the Seneca Chief from the lakes to the sea, a "mad author" writing history in opening the longest canal in all the world.

So the Towpath, that had been conceived amid ridicule and disbelief and born of vision, faith and determination, became a pathway of national destiny. New York became the Empire State. Western New York blossomed sturdily out of the swamps and the dark forests.

Thriving towns mushroomed on the banks of "Clinton's Folly." Rochester, an insignificant huddle beside the falls of the Genesee, burgeoned into "The Young Lion of the West," the fastest growing town in America. Medina, Albion, Holley, Newark, and all the "ports," Brockport, Spencerport, Fairport, came into being. Pittsford, Palmyra, Lyons, older villages, quickened to new commercial life when touched by the magic waters of a ditch 42 feet wide and four feet deep.

Now, after 120 years, the Empire State regards with benevolent tolerance the waterway that gave it greatness. The canal is a financial millstone about its neck, an aged pensioner who must be supported all of its days.

Yet in balancing up the account, the ledger shows that the state and Western New York owe the old Ditch a debt they can never repay.

*   *   *   *

When the 19th Century dawned, the canal bee was buzzing in many an American head.

The idea was not new. The Suez Canal was navigated by small craft as early as 600 B.C. The Romans built canals in Britain during their occupation of that isle. China dug her Imperial Waterway in 1289. The Italian De Vincis are credited with originating lockage in 1481. Europe saw a flurry of canal building in the 18th Century.

In 1792 the first canal was constructed in the United States, at South Hadley, Mass. That same year the Western Inland Lock Navigation Company was formed and soon had completed a three-mile, five-lock Little Falls Canal and another linking the Mohawk and Wood Creek.

But these were puny things compared with the great ditch of the Yorkers' dreams.

Many saw the vision. One was Cadwallader Colden, surveyor-general of the Province of New York, who as early at 1724 recorded the vague hope that Western New York, then a wilderness, might be penetrated by boat, independent of Lake Ontario.

Another was Gouverneur Morris, influential but impractical, who ventured the prediction that "at no distant day the great western seas will, by the aid of man, break through the barriers and mingle with the Hudson." But he believed natural gravity was the answer and did not realize the necessity of lockage.

In 1805 Jesse Hawley, who had been buying wheat in the Genesee Valley and conveying it by circuitous and uncertain routes to the Albany market, sat in the office of Colonel Mynderse at Seneca Falls and asked: "Why can't we have a canal?"

Mynderse retorted: "But where is your head of water?" Hawley strode to a map on the wall, traced with his finger Niagara Falls and Lake Erie and exclaimed: "There's your supply; there's your head of water."

The idea obsessed him and two years later, from his cell in the old Canandaigua jail where he was imprisoned for debt, Hawley wrote the 13 essays, which, under the name of Hercules, appeared in the Pittsburgh Commonwealth and the Genesee Messenger and fanned public sentiment for a waterway across the state.

There were formidable barriers to such a scheme. The Appalachian mountain chain stood athwart the path. Through the continental divide lay four natural passes, each an old Indian trail. The most northerly paralleled Lake Ontario and this was the route Hawley espoused. Lake Ontario was the more direct way but the young republic was then at sword's points with Britain, which ruled the lake's northern waters.

After the Revolution, land companies bought vast tracts in what is now Western New York. Pioneers, mainly of English ancestry, began making little clearings in the woods, rearing cabins, planting crops and founding scattered settlements.

But generally between the Hudson and Lake Erie stretched a forbidding tangle of swamp and forest. The only consequential towns west of the Mohawk were Batavia and Canandaigua, seats of the land companies. Roads were mere woods trails. The region was retarded by lack of transportation for marketing its products. Commerce generally followed the existing waterways southward to the port of Philadelphia. That was a long and expensive outlet to the sea.

Despite these difficulties, more and more covered wagons were rolling toward the setting sun, bound, not only for Western New York but also for Ohio and Michigan.

At the hour when from debtor's prison, Jess Hawley was sounding his call for a canal, the stage was set for the frontier to fulfil its destiny.

*   *   *   *

Hawley's call did not go unheard. In 1808 the first legislation was introduced at Albany for a survey of canal possibilities. A paltry sum was appropriated—but the seeds were sown.

Able James Geddes of Onondaga made the survey. He saw that Morris' idea of making the canal on one uniform level was impossible. The waterway must be adapted to the rise and fall of the land in a series of level stretches, each closed by a lock to allow vessels to be shifted from one level to another. Soon the red stakes of James Geddes were dotting the countryside. Other routes were proposed but the one Geddes chose in 1809 was almost the identical one the canal eventually pursued.

About that time, the greatest actor in the drama of the waterways came upon the stage. He became the canal's chief advocate. He mobilized and led its supporters through stormy years. His political fortunes were forever after associated with the fortunes of the Ditch. He was a six footer, a brilliant intellectual of aristocratic lineage. Sometimes he was brusque. He had little patience with sluggish minds. His foes termed him haughty. But he was a leader and he was a fighter.

His name was DeWitt Clinton, variously state senator, mayor of New York, United States senator, governor, and candidate for President.

Clinton fought down intrigue and calumny. He tasted temporary defeat. His enemies retired him to private life. They even kicked him off the board of canal commissioners. But Clinton used the canal issue as a springboard on which to bound back to political power. He fought, night and day, with voice and pen, for his Grand Canal. And when in 1825, after the Ditch was dug, he poured a keg of Lake Erie water into the Atlantic, it was DeWitt Clinton's greatest hour.

* * * *

On July 4, 1817, the first spadeful of earth for the Canal was turned at Rome.

The 362-mile waterway was dug, in three sections and under the contract system, in eight years at a cost of over seven million dollars. The Genesee was crossed at Rochester by an aqueduct that was the engineering marvel of the time. Across the valley of the Irondequoit was built a great embankment 70 feet high.

Bird's Eye View of Picturesque Medina

Albion, Proud "Queen of Orleans"

The strong arms and strong backs of thousands of sweating men built that Ditch across the state. Some Yankees and Yorkers wielded picks and shovels and trundled wheelbarrows. Some Southern Negroes wrought in the narrow prism.

But it was largely the Irish who dug the canal. They were fresh from the peat bogs, those men who sang strange Gaelic tunes as they doffed their breeches to plunge into Montezuma mire. They dwelt in fever-infested shacks, at the mercy of despotic bosses. They made only 50 to 75 cents a day. Disease, accidents and drunken brawls took their toll and the missionary priests in their rich brogue sang the Mass over many a fresh grave in the new land. Still the Irish dug on and inched the great Ditch westward until it tapped Erie water.

There were no steam shovels, no concrete mixers. Courage and back-breaking toil built the canal. But Yankee ingenuity played its role. When quicklime failed to slack properly, Canvass White of Utica developed a waterproof lime.

Because the cost of blasting powder was too high, a machine, manned by seven laborers and a team of horses or oxen, was devised to yank out 30 to 40 large stumps a day, a tremendous saving in manpower and time. Tall trees were brought down by means of a cable attached to their tops and wound by a wheel, attached to an endless screw. Horse scoops were brought into use. A plow with an additional sharp blade was perfected to cut through the smaller roots.

When the Erie Canal was done and a mighty column of traffic began to parade its shallow, narrow waters, it was truly said:

"They have built the longest canal in the world in the least time, with the least experience, for the least money and for the greatest public benefit."

*   *   *   *

I think the building of the Canal was the most significant

single event in the early history of the state and of this region. It also had far-reaching national import.

It forged an economic bond between the East and West that insured a Union victory when the Civil War came.

It built great cities, peopled great states, loosed a flood tide of immigration westward. It gave a rich frontier an outlet to the sea.

It made New York State an economic unit. It made New York City the commercial capital of the New World and ended the supremacy of Philadelphia.

It brought prosperity to the stunted backwoods of Western New York. It boosted the value of land. It cut the cost of freight from Rochester to Albany from $100 a ton to $10. Thirty-cent wheat in the Genesee Valley became dollar wheat. It reduced the time of travel between Buffalo and New York from six weeks to ten days.

And beyond question, the Canal made the cities of Rochester, Buffalo and Syracuse, as well as most of the smaller towns on its banks.

*   *   *   *

It made some fortunes too. Canal contracts formed the basis for a few. Boat building became big business. Every little town had its shipyard and all the basins swarmed with the vessels. Soon the mules and horses were bending their necks to the towlines of 4,000 canal boats. The horn of the boatmen kept the locktenders on the jump day and night. The weighlocks, those immense scales at the busiest ports, groaned under their burdens.

It was an era splashed with color. Thousands of men and boys took to the canal. They had to be tough—to stay on the Ditch. They drank, they swore, they fought—but they kept the canal boats churning Erie water and always "their hearts were young and gay."

At the outset the canal was not only a busy highway of trade. It also was a swank avenue of travel. The sleek, gaily painted packet boats, their horses a jingle with ivory rings and metal trimmings, gave the Ditch dash and color. The elite loitered on the decks of the packets in sunny weather and gave the Ditch tone. The arrival and departure of the passenger boats, which often were bitter rivals, were major events in canal towns of a century ago.

Elegant hotels rose beside the canal in the larger places, largely because sleeping accommodations were limited—and uncomfortable —on the packets.

Philip Hone of New York, the Lucius Beebe of his day, wrote in his diary in 1847:

"Canal traveling is pleasant enough in daytime but the sleeping is awful. The sleepers are packed on narrow shelves fastened to the side of the boat like dead pigs in a Cincinnati pork warehouse."

Those same packet boats in their time were crowded with men and women speaking many tongues, immigrants—German, Dutch, Scandinavian—seeking a new opportunity in a New World. Some of them stopped off in Western New York but the great majority went on to people the Midwest and contribute mightily to the progress of the nation.

The advent of the paralleling railroads in the 1840's and '50's sounded the knell of the passenger packets. The freighters survived the competition until the coming of the motor truck and the American mania for speed.

In the 1890's, almost every kind of craft, save lake schooners, plied the placid waters. Some were propelled by steam but most of them were mule-powered. Grain boats, heavily laden, eastward bound—empty ones scurrying back West for another cargo—tugs with the family wash flapping on the line—long, unwieldy timber rafts, the bane of the lock-keepers—freight steamers puffing along at ten miles an hour, taking on and discharging merchandise at every town—a few trim steam yachts and pleasure craft of less distinction tied up along the boat houses on the heelpath .... Clinton's Ditch was vibrantly alive 50 years ago.

Even as late as 1903, when the Barge Canal was born, there were 4,000 boats on the Canal, the majority owned by independents and most of them dependent on long-eared power. The ever-growing use of steam, the trend toward big corporations and the eventual demise of the Towpath changed all that.

The Barge Canal expansion was not the first "streamlining" for the waterway. Seven years after the Seneca Chief's maiden journey, the Ditch had to be enlarged. For thirty years the work went on. It was widened to 70 feet and deepened to seven feet. The locks were enlarged and in some places the curves of the course were eliminated. After 1862 the canal could carry 270-ton boats, instead of those weighing only 30 tons. This improvement cost the state a matter of thirty-one millions.

But let it be remembered, to the everlasting credit of the old canal, that when tolls were abolished in 1882, "Clinton's Folly" had earned forty-two million dollars over and above the original cost, expense of enlargement, maintenance and operation!

*　　　*　　　*　　　*

For nearly 30 years now, the Erie has been part of the state's Barge Canal system. Officially it's still the Erie but everybody speaks of the present ditch as the Barge.

The big improvement was authorized in 1903 over the vigorous opposition of the railroads. It cost the taxpayers 176 millions to build it, to say nothing of the heavy burden since of maintaining a toll-free waterway. It was widened to 125 feet (94 feet in cuts) and deepened to at least 12 feet in all places.

The Barge Canal was pronounced completed in 1918. Where the old ditch followed an artificial channel built by means of excavations and embankments, the modern one utilizes streams and lakes wherever feasible.

Generally it follows the route blazed so many years ago by Surveyor Geddes' red stakes. I saw at several points besides the present canal, clear traces of the two older routes—the Clinton ditch of 1825 and the enlarged Erie of 1832–1862. At Macedon water still flows in the second ditch. Still standing in a few places in this region are remains of locks built 120 years ago.

The most pronounced change in route hereabouts was in Rochester where the new waterway swings south of the city, crossing the river at Genesee Valley Park instead of by the old aqueduct downtown. Subway trains whizz by at breathtaking speed where crept the mule and horse-drawn barges of yesteryear.

*   *   *   *

You can't turn back the clock—save in your memories.

Not long ago I followed the old path, chopped by the imprints of countless hooves, through the towns that were mothered by Clinton's Ditch, from Medina in the orchard country to Clyde in the land of the drumlins.

Whenever I spoke of the old canal, its mules, its "hoggies," its weighlocks, its heelpath, tired eyes sparkled and voices softened by nostalgic memories, would murmur:

"I can see them now, as if it were only yesterday."

That yesterday was a pleasant one on the banks of the Erie.

Many a man, no longer young, would say: "Why, I learned to swim in the Canal."

They hold in fond remembrance long gone summers when the old ditch was their swimming hole and fishing ground; winters when it was their skating rink.

There are memories, too, of excursions and picnic parties on the quiet waters.

So on the ledger, along with all the figures and dollar signs, there is jotted down a sentimental entry to the credit of the Grand Canal.

Rock-Ribbed Town

MY "Canal Zone" began at Medina. Before I left Rochester by tugboat for that Orleans County port, western terminus of my Towpath trek, I was told that:

"You will find Medina a mighty busy, substantial, friendly town. But you won't find anything unusual there."

Evidently my informant was no follower of the Robert L. Ripley "Believe It or Not" newspaper feature. Twice in recent years has the name of Medina, N. Y. appeared in that amazing compilation of the unusual, gathered from all corners of the earth.

Once the Ripley caption read: "A road runs under the Erie Canal at Medina, N. Y."

The other time it was: "A church stands in the middle of a street at Medina, N. Y."

Culvert Road is the name of the highway that pierces the high embankment east of the village. At that point Erie water courses over a concrete bottom.

"The church in the middle of a street" is St. John's Episcopal and the street is Church Street. The 118-year old edifice stands squarely in that thoroughfare just before Church Street joins East Center Street. There the street splits, with either fork bypassing the historic brown stone church.

I found also at Medina the most picturesque scenery encountered on my Towpath ramble. Of necessity a canal generally follows level country. And flat lands are seldom picturesque.

But in the very heart of Medina, the frothing waters of the Oak Orchard Creek tumble over a 15-foot fall, set in a rugged chasm that is a miniature Genesee Gorge.

Man has enhanced the impressiveness of the scene with a massive aqueduct and high retaining walls to carry the winding canal across the ravine. Man also has harnessed the waters of the Oak Orchard for electric power and made a little lake called Glenwood, north of the village, before the stream joins the far mightier lake called Ontario.

I did find Medina, just as described in advance, "mighty busy, substantial and friendly."

But commonplace? Hardly.

*   *   *   *

Medina's history is unusual—in that it goes back some 40 million years, quite a spell in any reckoning.

In that distant day, in what the geologists call the Silurian period, the waters of the great ocean covered all this region. The ancient sea was shallow along what is now Lake Ontario. Little by little, streams deposited sand grains in the watery depths. Those grains merged and solidified through the centuries until, when at last the salt waters receded, they remained, deep down in the bed of the erstwhile sea, in the form of the enduring rock that geologists and builders the world over know as the Medina sandstone.

Erosion gradually cut away the tons of rock that overhung the sandstone until the Medina strata lay just beneath the surface, waiting only the probing hands of the men who dug the Erie Canal.

Dr. J. Edward Hoffmeister, eminent University of Rochester geologist, explained that the Medina underlies this whole area. At

Letchworth Park it is down 3,000 feet. It tinges with red the walls of Rochester's river gorge. It extends from Buffalo eastward across the state to beyond Syracuse. It ranges in color from light gray to reddish brown, with variegated hues as well.

Because in Orleans County, the ancient sea was shallow, the sandstone was nearest the surface there and most easily brought out. That is why an almost continuous line of quarries sprang up along the Clinton Ditch from Medina to Holley, to maintain for 80 years an industry that made the name of Medina famous in many lands.

* * * *

The first settlers came to the Medina region so long ago their identity is difficult to trace.

Archeologists for years have been fascinated by the remains of an ancient fortification, enclosing a three-acre circular tract and bordered by a moat or trench, some three miles south of Medina.

From the many relics uncovered there, Dr. Arthur C. Parker, director of the Rochester Museum and a foremost authority on Indian lore, believes "Fort Shelby" was built by "pre-Confederation Iroquois" who dwelt there before Hiawatha welded the Big Five into a League of Nations.

Dr. Parker also points out that while the Red Men may have built the embankment to repel human enemies, it is also probable the fort was to protect the settlement against the bears, wolves, panthers and wildcats that roamed the wilderness.

* * * *

Visit the Orleans countryside in the blossom scented springtime when the orchards are one vast tent of pink and white or in harvest time when they—and the rich black mucklands—yield their stupendous bounty and you find it hard to believe that this fertile plain was once the most forbidding and desolate of landscapes.

But nowhere were the woods thicker, the swamps more deadly with fever germs, the frontier more isolated, the roads rougher. Yet land-hungry settlers, mostly of the English stock, pressed on into that wilderness.

They bought tracts, with little down payment, from a Dutch syndicate, the Holland Land Company, which had acquired 3,600,000 acres in the western end of the state. That vast holding was called the Holland Purchase, with Batavia as its capital.

Shelby Center to the southward was founded in 1803 and salt works were established at the brine springs near the present Medina soon after, but there was no Medina—until the Grand Canal came.

The first buildings were those hastily thrown up along the red stakes of Geddes' surveyors, to house the canal diggers. In 1823 Ebenezer Mix, pioneer surveyor and shrewd business man, laid out the village which was named Medina, probably after the sacred city where rest the bones of Mohammed, the Prophet.

There's another tale, undoubtedly apocryphal, about the town's name. It concerns a boarder at the pioneer tavern of Uri Moore, who had a servant named Dinah. This man, entirely by mistake, opened the door of Dinah's room one night. She screamed out in fright. The boarder retreated in confusion, calling out "It's me, Dinah." Others in the house heard the remark. "Me, Dinah," became a byword in the little settlement and according to the legend, gave the place its name.

When in 1824 the Ditch was opened from Brockport to Lockport and flat-bottomed passenger and freight boats began to ply the shallow waters, Medina burst into bloom. The houses that had been built to shelter canal diggers were taken over by more permanent settlers. More dwellings, warehouses, stores sprang up, mostly around the docks. Prosperity came to the countryside, emerging from the woods and swamps, for now the farmers had a road to market—the Canal.

The 1830's were boom days in Medina. In 1835 the Eagle Tavern, three stories high and of stone, with a gilded bird atop its belfry, arose beside the Canal. It was the most pretentious hostelry in the region. It had two bar rooms, one, well appointed, on the main floor, catering to the gentry, and a plainer one, in the basement where common folk gulped down the native whisky—at 3 cents a glass. The hotel burned down in 1841.

And it was in the lush 1830's that the quarrying industry was born.

* * * *

That industry, like the village itself, was an offspring of the Canal.

When Artemas Allen snared the contract for building the canal aqueduct across the Oak Orchard gorge, the plan was to haul the stone all the way from Canandaigua. Allen began nosing around the gorge and found right on the spot far better stone for the job than any Canandaigua could offer. The water lime that went into the aqueduct was made from stone burned in log heaps and ground with an upright revolving stone.

Word spread of the abundant stone deposits. In 1837, John Ryan, who came to Orleans County on foot from Williamsport, Pa., opened the first quarry in the Medina area.

Soon the canal banks, within the confines of Orleans County, were lined with pits. The first stone cutters were English. Later the Irish went into the quarries. Then the Poles came and much later, the Italians. Medina became a melting pot for many racial stocks and assimilated them all. The Poles and Italians remained after the quarries closed, to form considerable segments of the community.

It was the English quarrymen who built St. John's Church, (at first it was called St. Luke's), out of the native sandstone. In the beginning the foundations were roofed over to provide a place of worship. Little by little the stone cutters built, in their spare time, the stately edifice that stands today, after 118 years, "in the middle of a street."

There's a tall tale that in the early days a prankish wind blew the oblong-shaped stone tower slightly off its base and that while the flock was considering ways of righting it, another wind blew it back securely into its old position.

For many years Attorney Leroy J. Skinner was associated with the quarrying interests in the area. None knows better the history of that industry's rise and fall.

The heyday of the quarries was in the decade that began in 1890. The collapse came around 1912. At the turn of the century there were 50 of them in the county and 2,000 acres of sandstone quarrying lands. At first virtually all the stone was shipped by canal. The great slabs, blasted out by gunpowder, were hoisted by derricks on to flat-bottomed boats, open at the center. After 1853 when the Falls Line of the New York Central was built, considerable stone was transported by rail.

Astute, historically minded Lawyer Skinner looked out the window of his office and in fancy saw again, after some 30 years, the long swing wagons hauling the slabs up Main Street to the freight house.

Those wagons rumble no more; most of the old quarries are full of water in which swim many fish. Nobody can figure out how they got there.

But the staunch Medina rock can be found almost anywhere. It is in Sibley College of Cornell University. It is in Anderson Hall and in Sibley Library on the old University of Rochester Campus. It is in the Federal Building in Rochester's Church Street; in the harbor breakwaters of Buffalo and Cleveland; in the pillars of the

Brooklyn, George Washington and Williamsburg bridges; in the steps of the State Capitol at Albany.

Rochester's graceful old St. Patrick's Cathedral, now torn down, was built of the gray Medina. In Rochester's Main Street, down under the more modern paving, are the old Medina blocks. They went, too, into Cleveland's busy Euclid Avenue and into the streets of Havana, Cuba, after the war of '98.

Everywhere in Medina you see the stone that made its name famous. It's in her City Hall and in her State Armory. There's hardly a wooden building in the business district. Even those of brick have sills and copings of the sandstone. There's a house in Bates Road whose entire floor is one solid block of Medina.

Around 1900 Skinner was a leading spirit in a move to consolidate the 50 independent quarries into a cohesive unit. It was not a success. Then a powerful rival, Portland cement, came into the picture. One by one the once busy quarries along the Ditch closed down.

Leroy Skinner told how early religious exhorters used to call the town "a city founded on a rock."

Pioneer blood flows in his veins. His father came to Orleans County in 1830 on a packet, he recalled, adding that, "My father often told of people going westward on the canal in home-made flat-bottomed boats with their families and goods, tugging the boats by hand along from the old towpath. Sometimes the good-natured canallers would allow the prospectors to hitch on behind their boats."

I had a chat with another long-time resident of Medina. His name is Charles D. Hood and the sign on his office door says "insurance." He was for years a newspaper correspondent and was once a publisher. Charley Hood has flowing white hair, an old-fashioned flowing white mustache and an old-fashioned flowing black tie.

He also has an old-fashioned courtesy and kindliness to strangers.

He, too, has seen many changes in the village. He remembers boyhood fights with the Irish lads on "Paddy Hill," busy days at the docks when hundreds of barrels of apples were hauled by canal; when there were 10 passenger trains daily on the Falls Road. Now there is one a day each way. He spoke with nostalgia of the interurbans of the Rochester, Lockport & Buffalo Railway. One can still see the old tracks peeking out from under the paving at downtown corners.

When the Million Dollar Highway wound its way through the fruit belt, the trucks and autos sounded the doom of the interurban cars.

Hood recalled colorful times in Medina in the heyday of the quarries and of the canal, when there were some 35 saloons in the village. Mix quarrymen, canallers and transient fruit pickers, stir well with alcohol on a Saturday night and you have a steaming dish for the constabulary.

I found another Medinian who is steeped in local lore. But I had to seek him out in Rochester. Russell Waldo, a veteran newspaper man, at present is holding a responsible job with the Bausch and Lomb plant although he retains his home in Medina.

He told me about Andrew Downey and his circus. Downey is dead and his circus was absorbed years ago by the Sparks shows, but many an oldtimer will remember when the show boats, built in Medina, and with "Downey Bros. Shows" painted boldly across their sides, sailed the Ditch and pitched their tents in every canal town. That was shortly after the turn of the century. Maybe oldtimers in Clyde "way down east" on the waterway, will remember when Andrew Downey, armed with a tent stake, acquitted himself creditably in the face of a near riot.

You can't travel 20 miles in any direction in these parts without coming across a bridge or a road that the late William "Dude" Gallagher built. He began as a mail carrier and became a contractor of note. Today his name lives in an important trucking company.

Medina beats no drums nor does it concern itself unduly with its past: It is one of the briskest towns I found along the Towpath and the hum of industry fills the air.

It has five iron works, two furniture factories, two large canneries, among its industries, besides being the center of a rich fruit and vegetable region. When the quarries gave up the ghost, Medina did not shrivel and die. It went on making other things. For did not the old exhorters, when speaking of Medina take this text from the book of Matthew.

"And the rain descended and the floods came and the winds blew and beat upon that house; and it fell not, for it was founded on a rock."

* * * *

The rock-ribbed village, according to its 1945 boosters, numbers 6,200 souls. The Federal Census of 1940 puts the figure at 5,871.

Medina has a daily newspaper, the Journal. It has had one for 60 years, probably the smallest town in the state to boast a daily.

East of Medina is Knowlesville, also born of the Clinton Ditch. It was named after its first settler, William Knowles, who cleared land there in 1815. Three years later canal surveyors pitched their tents—and drove their stakes—on Knowles' land. In 1825 settlement began; first, a house or two; then a warehouse; a tavern and Knowlesville emerged as a thriving early canal port. The first boat load of wheat ever shipped from Orleans County came out of the now somnolent port of Knowlesville.

* * * *

I was not the only stranger in Medina that bright but chilly day before Memorial Day.

Bands were playing martial airs and Main Street resounded to the rat-tat-a-tat of machine gunfire. For Medina was host to the "Here's Your Infantry Show," starring 80 young overseas veterans. They set up their bazookas, their machine-guns and their other Jap killers on the principal street. People poured in from Knowlesville, from Albion, from Waterport, from Middleport, from all over the region. That night a sham battle on the outskirts drew a great throng.

But amid all the fanfare, Medina characteristically never lost sight of the real objective of the spectacle—the Seventh War Loan.

A War Bond contest was being waged in the village school. If the kids made their quota, they'd get the afternoon off.

That afternoon the streets swarmed with school kids.

And on every Medina lip, the talk was not so much about the warriors and their weapons, although they evoked much admiration, but rather about the way the school children had done themselves and the village proud in accounting for nearly $4,500 in War Bonds.

Verily, Medina, child of the Clinton Ditch, "is a house founded upon a rock."

It is the rock of an exalted community spirit.

Queen of Orleans

FAR in the distance, something silvery gleamed above the green of the trees.

The man at the wheel of the canal tugboat said: "That's Albion ahead. That's the Courthouse dome that shines."

Circling that glistening dome like a guard of honor, "the clustered spires of Albion stand," to paraphrase an old verse about an older town.

The canaller went on: "You know, one night when we laid over in Albion, I took a stroll around the town. There wasn't much night life and the main stem was pretty quiet. But the place's got something. Atmosphere, I guess you'd call it. There's an old red Courthouse in a shady square with churches and old mansions, like you see in New England and the South, all around it. It kinda gives you a feeling of history and class— if you know what I mean."

I think I know what he meant. I get that same feeling every time I visit the canal-born county seat town in the orchard country. I think the canal man put it very well: "History and class." A more stilted phrase would be "An air of consequence."

Albion, like the older shire towns of Canandaigua and Batavia, has a touch of the grand manner, born of past glories. The shining Courthouse dome is a symbol, not only of her status as the seat of county government, but also of her proud memories.

For in this stately village under its canopy of old trees, lived men who in their time played colorful and important roles in the history of the state and nation. Here mighty financial enterprises were spawned, strong politics brewed, traditions born, fortunes made—and lost.

Albion is the queen of Orleans and her throne is the Courthouse Square where ever echo the distant drums of history.

* * * *

That square was Albion's cradle. It was there in 1811 that doughty William McCollister raised a log hut, the first dwelling on the site of the present village. Neighbors were few and far between and life was lonely in the backwoods. When the next year McCollister's wife sickened and died, there were no boards for her coffin. So the settlers hewed and split planks from the standing trees for a rough box. There was no minister so a neighbor read the burial service.

Around 1802, Joseph Ellicott, agent for the Holland Land Company, visioned a busy port on Lake Ontario at the mouth of the Oak Orchard and laid out a village there which he called Manila. He built a highway along an old Indian trail from that point to Batavia. Ellicott's port never materialized but Albion's Main Street today follows the road Ellicott built.

After McCollister, a handful of other pioneers built cabins amid the mud and stumps.

Then Clinton's Ditch was dug and breathed life into the tiny settlement. A thriving town, which her settlers called Newport, sprang up on the banks of the Erie.

When in 1825 De Witt Clinton rode the Seneca Chief from Lake Erie to the Atlantic at the completion of the Grand Canal, his flotilla passed through Newport in the night and the townspeople sat up for the celebration and hired two fiddlers that they might dance away the waiting hours.

Joseph B. Achilles, Orleans County historian, has found out that the cannon, which lined the entire length of the canal to relay the salute to Clinton's triumphant parade, were captured from the British by Perry in the Battle of Lake Erie. They were taken from the government depot at Erie, Pa., to the Brooklyn Naval Station, to be scattered by boats along the canal for the celebration of its opening. One of Joe Achilles' many historical objectives is to find out what finally became of those guns.

* * * *

In 1824 it was decided to form a new county out of the fast-growing northeastern part of the Holland Purchase. A dispute arose over its name. The followers of John Quincy Adams wanted their leader honored. The cohorts of Old Hickory wanted it called Jackson. A compromise was evolved and the new county was given the picturesque Old World name of Orleans.

Then came the fight over the county seat between Newport and Gaines. It's an oft-told tale how Newporters wined and dined the commissioners who came to pick the site; how they showed them a busy mill with wheels turned by a swiftly flowing stream. It was a shrewd trick. A few days before the mill had been idle and Sandy Creek dry. The creek had been dammed and the mill wheel set to going to impress the commissioners. So it was that Gaines lost the county seat to its younger, smaller rival.

Because there was another Newport in the state, the name of the growing canal town was changed in 1828 to Albion, the ancient name for England, meaning "white." Maybe the pioneers of English ancestry who renamed the village were thinking of the chalky cliffs of Dover in the mother land.

The eventful year of 1828 also saw the opening of the first Albion stone quarry. The industry was the commercial backbone of Albion for nearly a century. Once a huge slab from the Brady quarry was loaded on a flat boat and taken to Albany to become the top stone of the State Capitol's steps. Albionites will tell you their town had more quarries than Medina. Medinans will tell you their stone was superior. The rivalry was intense. It does not matter any more. The once busy quarries along the canal are nearly all deserted now.

In 1833 Caroline Phipps borrowed $4,000 and Phipps Union Seminary, a day and boarding school for young ladies, began its long stay on the Square. In 1837 the Albion Academy was organized.

The young queen of Orleans was assuming a cultural tone.

Two early merchants, R. S. and Lorenzo Burrows, founders of a family long influential in the village, built a brick block that still stands after 120 years, with its curious little offices and stores facing the canal. They brought the first one-horse spring wagons to the region. Previously there had been only sleds and lumber wagons.

A more elegant era had dawned for Albion.

As the years went by, the town gained financial and political prestige. The Heelpath on the south side was lined with warehouses, stores and grog shops. The Towpath, opposite, was jammed with mules and horses hauling the produce of a growing land. In 1853 the railroad came, to give a new transportation outlet for the quarry-orchard country.

In 1859 Albion was the scene of a catastrophe. As a feature of the county fair, a Brockport daredevil advertised he would walk a tight rope across the canal. So many crowded the bridge in the village to watch the spectacle that the span gave way, plunging 250 persons into the water. Fifteen bodies, mostly of young people, were taken from the wreckage of the bridge.

Fortunes were being made in Albion. Her financiers invested heavily in the International Bridge at Niagara Falls; the quarries and the orchards flourished. The quality folk out South Main Street bought finer carriages and smarter horses, hired coachmen-gardeners, built ice houses and new cottages at the lake. Albion's political bosses made their influence felt in state party councils.

The queen was sitting grandly on her throne.

*   *   *   *

The quarries brought a racial mixture; first the Yorkshiremen who spoke an English barely intelligible to Western New Yorkers; then the Irish, later the Poles, and finally the Italians. The Poles today have a sizeable colony, not so large as Medina's, but they maintain their own church. The Italians are more numerous and form a considerable portion of Albion's 4,660 population (1940 census).

After the quarries closed, things were quieter along Erie water. More and more retired farmers came to live in town. Death and financial reverses left their mark on South Main Street. Some of the mansions were torn down; others passed out of the hands of the Old Families.

But don't get the idea that Albion today is any deserted village. It is in the heart of one of the state's richest fruit, tomato and pea producing belts. It is the trading center for a large rural area. It has an extensive canning and food industry.

Above all it has the old traditions. They will never die.

When Uncle Sam sought to build a concrete monstrosity of a postoffice near the square, the village fought successfully for a building in keeping with its dignified and historic surroundings. Good taste always has been a hallmark of the Albion scene.

I mentioned to an old resident plans of a canning company for a major expansion in the frozen food field and wondered if "that would not help Albion?"

The old resident gave me a sharp glance and there was a touch of scorn in his voice as he replied: "It might make Albion BUSIER, if that is what you mean."

Main Street merchants may not share his views. But in old towns like Albion there persists in many hearts the unorthodox idealogy that mere bigness, bustle and material growth are not the Alpha and Omega of life.

* * * *

What of the dramatis personae who have trod the Albion stage?

Joe Achilles dug up from his treasure trove of local history an advertisement dated 1853. It read:

"Having completed extensive arrangements for manufacturing and greatly enlarging warerooms at Nos. 4 and 5 Clark's Block, we now offer a large and elegant assortment of cabinet furniture, mattresses, etc., of superior workmanship.—We are also prepared to furnish coffins and a good hearse and carriage."

In big letters was the firm's name: G. M. PULLMAN & CO.

Yes, it was the same George M. Pullman who became a titan of industry, who founded the sleeping car company that bears his name. But in 1853 he was a young cabinet maker in Albion. He helped his father move buildings, too, and that year took a contract to remove certain structures that obstructed the enlargement of the Erie Canal. Five years later he left for Chicago and began work on his pioneer sleeping "palace."

His parents are buried in Mount Albion Cemetery and one of the six churches within a radius of two blocks from the Courthouse is the Pullman Memorial (Universalist) Church, his gift to the town in which he lived as a young man.

Another young man left Albion before the Civil War. His name was Rufas Bullock, and he went South to Atlanta, where he became an express company executive. During the war that antebellum carpetbagger was acting quartermaster general of the Confederate Army and in reconstruction days was elected governor of Georgia. His reign was short and stormy. When Negro members were expelled from the legislature, he petitioned Congress for their restoration. He was repudiated in the next election, resigned his office and hurried North. He later returned to Georgia and became a railroad president and textile manufacturer. In 1902 he came back to Albion to spend the rest of his days.

At one time the upstate leaders of both political parties were Albion men. The Republican was Noah Davis and the Democrat was Sanford E. Church. Both were lawyers and jurists. Davis presided over the trial of William M. Tweed in 1873 and sentenced that Tammany grafter to 12 years in prison and fined him $12,000. The sentence later was overturned on a technicality but nevertheless Tweed died in Ludlow Street jail. Judge Davis also presided at the trial of Ned Stokes for the murder of Jim Fisk, New York's most sensational case of the 1870s.

Judge Church was the second of his name to attain distinction in politics and the law. He served as lieutenant governor of New York as well as state chief justice. He once received some complimentary votes for the Democratic presidential nomination at a national convention. A grandson carries on the family name and tradition in Albion. And the noble old white colonial home of the Churches, near the Courthouse Square, is one of the town's showplaces.

Elizur K. Hart was the son of a pioneer and in his time a financial power. He was a director of the International Bridge Company, a banker, one of the few Democrats ever elected to Congress from the district and an one time co-owner of the Rochester Post Express. The huge turreted Hart mansion has been torn down but on from 1811, when Joseph Hart settled in the wilds, the family has been one of consequence in Albion.

Years ago a youth with a superb tenor voice tended bar briefly in Albion. His name was Chauncey Olcott.

"Ask Mr. Foster" was a household word some 30 years ago. The man who originated it and the travel and information bureau of which it was a symbol was an Albion native. Ward Foster left his father's hat store in the village to open a pharmacy in New York and eventually to found the agency that had branches all over the world. In one year three million people "asked Mr. Foster."

Albion also was the birthplace of Actor William Hodge, who starred in humorous roles. Albion people recall, a little wryly, how when Hodge was playing at the old Lyceum in Rochester, they sent a delegation to the city with a big floral piece to honor the native son. Hodge made a speech thanking the "people of Rochester" for their tribute and never mentioned Albion.

Of late years a man from Albion has attracted national notice—in an unusual field. He is Charles W. Howard, probably the best known Santa Claus in America. He was born and still lives on the farm that has been in his family since Holland Purchase days. When he was in fourth grade, he was picked, because of his chubby and cherubic countenance, to play a Santa Claus role. He's been doing it ever since. He likes children and he likes to make toys so the role came natural to him. For nine years he was a department store Santa in Rochester and Buffalo. He was so successful that he was asked to teach other Santas his technique. So he opened a school in his Albion home. In 1938 he stepped into the national limelight when he conducted a "Santa Claus College" in Santa Claus, Ind. Among his pupils were James Cagney and Edward C. Robinson of Hollywood, Calif.

*   *   *   *

Dr. Benjamin Howes is hardly a national figure but he is a colorful one locally. This former Army veterinarian, who rides like a Cossack, although he is in his seventies, lives at nearby Carlton. There he has a remarkable collection of agricultural and kitchen implements going back to frontier times. Straight and trim, he is a familiar figure on horseback in all Albion parades and celebrations.

There's Charley Palmer, who spends much of his time digging for Indian relics, particularly in the Shelby area and who has many friends among the Tonawanda Reservation Indians. His barn in Albion houses many trophies, including rare Indian pottery.

Albion is a different sort of town. Her people have varied interests. Go to the Town Club where the business and professional men meet for luncheon and you hear talk that is not confined to the weather, the prospects of the tomato and apple crops or village gossip.

You will hear about the gallows on which the last man was hanged in Orleans County back in the 1880's and which now reposes in the attic of the jail; about the old Opera House and the stars who played there; about the old canal days when boys who are now grown men used to throw stones at the mule drivers just to hear them curse; of the freight packet Frankie Reynolds, that stopped at every canal town with its cargo of groceries, hardware and beer.

* * * *

In Barre Center, four miles south of Albion, there's an old brick and frame house that once was a tavern and that contains a hidden staircase and a hidden room.

When the present owners, Mr. and Mrs. Carl Hakes, took over the property, they were no little surprised on opening what they took to be a cupboard door, to find steep, cowbwebby stairs leading up to the attic. And at the end of the stairway is a brick walled cell in the middle of the upper room under the ridge pole.

The answer to the mystery probably is the Underground Railway by which fugitive Negro slaves were spirited to freedom across the Canadian border in pre Civil War days.

* * * *

It's quite a hike, at least a mile and a half, out to George MacFarland's place on the Butts Road east of the village. But I felt it was worth it.

MacFarland, in his ninetieth year, with broad shoulders and

blue Irish eyes that look searchingly into yours, is probably the last of the old time quarrymen. When he was a young lad, he drove mules hauling his brother's boat from Albion to Albany and return. One trip was enough. "I never was so glad to see the Courthouse dome at Albion as when that was over," he said.

He began his half century of quarrying in the early 1870's as waterboy in one of the Albion pits. All day long he heard little but Gaelic spoken by the gang he served. Then he became a stone cutter and in 1877 went to the Ohio quarries. Twenty years later he returned to Albion. The industry then was its zenith along the Canal. MacFarland stayed in the quarries until they closed.

He told of the live frog the stone cutters found when they split a great slab years ago. "Some people thought the frog had been there thousands of years. Others said it never happened; that we made it up. But I saw it with my own eyes. I think it is easily explained. There was a crevice in the stone and water coursed through it. The frog might have passed into the fissure when tiny. He may have lived there only a matter of months or a few years. But he was there all right and it caused a lot of talk in the quarries at the time."

MacFarland looked out toward the canal. "Once there seemed to be tows passing all the time. Now you rarely see one," he said.

He remembers wild nights in the now so serene village. "You could hardly go uptown nights when I was young without seeing two or three fights. Sometimes they were mass battles when the stonecutters came down from Medina looking for trouble. They generally found it."

"One night—I think it was Fair time or the Fourth of July—there were lots of people in town. A big farmer from Waterport was full of hard cider and challenging everybody in sight. In one set-to, he lost his hat. I picked it up. It was a fine black felt and I thought I'd be decent enough to hand it to him. I made my way through the crowd to the Waterport bully. He was crazy drunk. Without a word he hit me a blow that almost knocked me down. I was young and pretty husky those days.

"The bully was standing in front of a many-paned store window; I let him have it and he went bang through that window, but not before he had torn my Sunday coat nearly to shreds. The sheriff picked him up and put him in the lockup. When he sobered up, I refused to press charges—when he agreed to pay for my torn coat. We became good friends after that."

George MacFarland did not say who paid for the window.

* * * *

In the evening my friend, Morris Wright, drove me up to Eagle Harbor on the canal just west of Albion.

We passed along a street where the old trolley tracks that led to the abandoned Fair Grounds still are visible. The Albion Fair once drew people from all over the countryside. Changing times and the popularity of the automobile killed it, as they have so many other fairs. But Albion men still fancy good horseflesh and several trotters are stabled on the otherwise deserted grounds.

Nearby is the State Training School, for mentally defective women. It was opened in 1893 as the Western House of Refuge for Women. It has about 300 inmates. The school is so sequestered and aloof from the village that its presence causes hardly a ripple in the community.

We stopped before a lovely Colonial farmhouse on a hill above Eagle Harbor. There Mark Cole lives. He is an unusual personality with many interests. A former member of the State Assembly, he is now attached to the Internal Revenue Bureau.

The home in which he lives has been in his family for more than a century. His grandfather, Charles A. Danolds, looks down from the wall of the high-ceilinged, spacious living room. Danolds had a contract for work on enlargement of the old Erie Ditch. As an old, old man, he saw the work begun on the Barge Canal.

Mark Cole recalled that then the old man said "Give me some of my Irish diggers with picks and shovels and wheelbarrows and they'd do a better job than all this machinery."

Eagle Harbor once was quite a port with mills and docks and warehouses. Cole remembered when canal boats would lay up there for the winter and the mules and horses would be stabled in the neighborhood.

Cole collects many unusual things. He gave me "A Poetical Geography and Arithmetic in Verse," all in rhyme. He has a little book with "Thomas Jefferson" written on the flyleaf in the authenticated handwriting of the Sage of Monticello.

* * * *

When I left Albion by bus early the next morning, I cast a parting glance at the silvery dome shining above the trees of Courthouse Square.

"History and class" the canal man had said of Albion.

He was right as rain.

On the Square

I THINK there is nothing so American about America as her villages of the 1,000-1,500 population class.
Their name is legion. They are on the rocky sea coasts, on the treeless plains, amid the wooded hills, on the banks of the proud rivers and the nameless creeks—and beside the still waters of the Erie Canal.

They exude peace and a sense of restfulness. They keep green a serene and unhurried way of life that our fathers knew. They raise few racial or class barriers. They accept a person for what he is. He is a neighbor, clothed in the dignity of his individuality, not an atom tossed about in a sea of other atoms. They approach the democracy of the American Dream.

In such villages, under spreading old trees, jaded folk may, for a little time, escape the sound and fury of urban "civilization," the pushing, callously impersonal crowds, the reeking motor fumes, the incessant, often senseless, race against time.

Now I don't have in mind one of those gone-to-seed, tumble down places already in the clutch of rigor mortis. I am thinking of a village that pulses with life, whose curbs are lined with farmers' cars; whose high school resembles a baronial castle; whose fire hall is replete with shiny, modern apparatus; whose pride is bound-

Street Scene—Holley 50 Years Ago

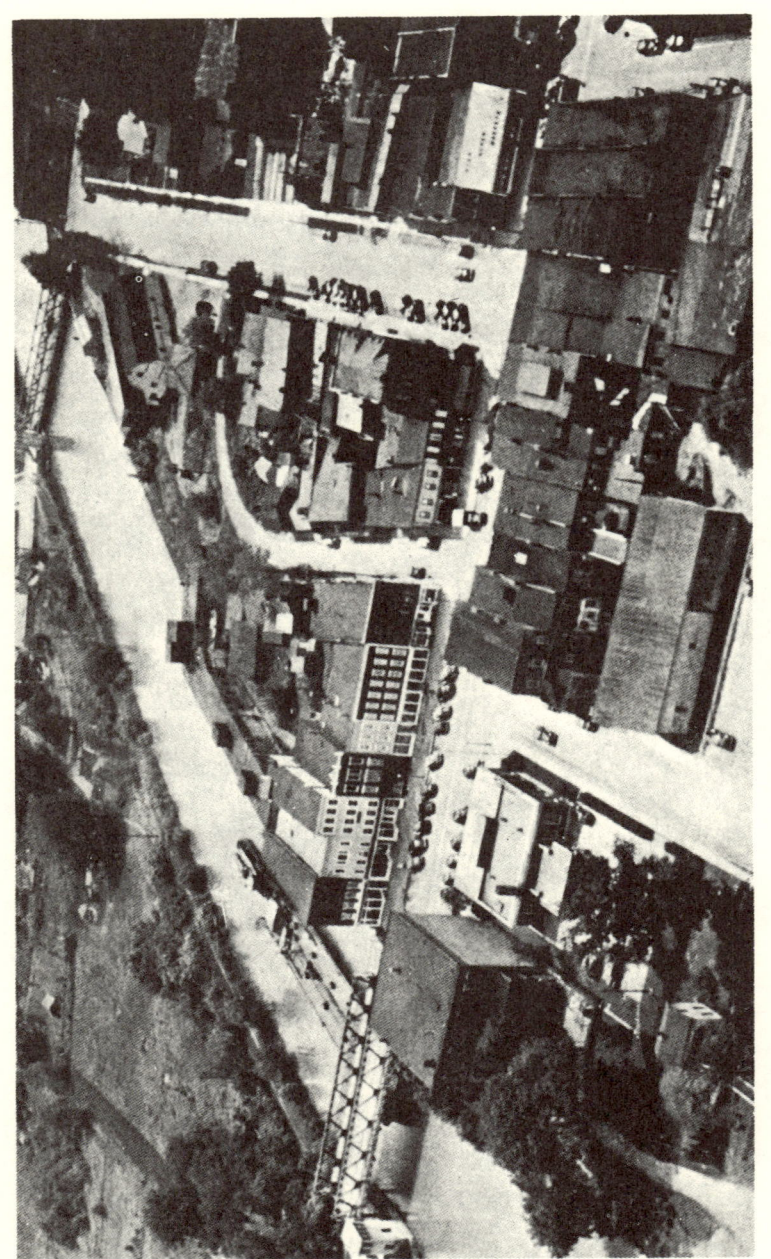

Busy Brockport, Born of the Canal

less in its athletic teams, bands, volunteer fire department, veterans' posts and churches.

Of course, I have in mind a particular community as a symbol of those thousands of others that just get under the four-figure wire in the census derby.

This particular village has a distinctive public square, green with shrubs. The business places of the town flank it on four sides. At its head in a tall church tower the village clock ticks off the long years. It is a little bit of old England in the pleasant and typically American orchard country of Western New York, beside the Ditch that Clinton built 120 years ago.

The village's very name brings to mind bright red berries, green leaves and Christmas time although they have naught to do with its name.

Like a convention orator, I've kept you in suspense too long. It is time to name my candidate.

Ladies and gentlemen, I give you Holley, N. Y.

*   *   *   *

In the beginning there was only the shadowy hemlock forest where stands the village today.

Holley is in the township of Murray at the eastern rim of the county of Orleans. In 1812 Stephen Lewis and William Rice made the first clearing in what is now Holley. Two years later John Reed had 16 kettles going at his salt works at the old deerlick near a tiny settlement called Saltport.

In 1817, when the Grand Canal's route was assured, sagacious Aerovester Hamlin bought 100 acres there. In 1822 he laid out a village around the square. He visioned shops and dwellings lining three sides and canal docks and warehouses on the east. Then there were only six buildings in the settlement. But when the Ditch was completed through Saltport in 1823, things began to hum in the clearing and Hamlin's dream came true. He built a mansion on an eminence east of the canal where he could watch the busy docks and square.

The salt works languished and died. The hemlock forest was transformed into a multitude of logs floated off on canal rafts. The name of the village was changed from Saltport to Holley in honor of Myron Holley, one of the fathers of the canal. He never lived in the village that bears his name. He was variously a resident of Canandaigua, of Lyons and of Rochester, where he died.

Myron Holley fought for the canal beside De Witt Clinton in the stirring legislative battles of 1817–18. When their fight was won, he became a canal commissioner and no man played a greater role, save Clinton, in its construction. He rode on horseback from place to place, sleeping wherever night overtook him, in workers' shanties, in vermin-infested inns, under the stars. He cast up his involved accounts by candlelight. After the canal was built, his enemies had the Legislature call him on the carpet for an unaccounted $30,000, out of all the millions he had handled. In the end Holley's integrity was vindicated.

He was a warrior in many camps, a leader in the anti-Masonic and the temperance movements, a man of outspoken views. But above all, he was a powerful figure in building the canal and it is fitting that today a canal town bears his name.

*   *   *   *

The quarries were opened and the railroad came to enhance Holley's prosperity. The orchards flourished and the farmers made the good earth do their bidding. In the early days, all the village's commercial tides eddied around the Clinton Ditch.

In 1856 the bank of the canal gave way and the waters poured into Card's Gulf, sweeping away a boat and taking one life. In 1866 fire ravaged the business district on the square.

When in 1856 the canal was enlarged, the route was changed to its present course north of the village. But the old Clinton Ditch stayed for half a century as a slip connecting the newer canal with lumber yards and warehouses in the town. An old drawing in the weekly Standard office, shows the village in panorama with its main waterway and tributary, giving Holley a Venice-like aspect.

The old slip carried pleasure craft, as well as cargoes of lumber and grain. When the Rochester, Lockport and Buffalo trolley line was built and the Barge Canal expansion was begun, it was abandoned. But the outlines of the ditch are still visible, back of the stores on the east side of the square. A stone house, still standing east of the old ditch and known as the Miller place, was once a canal grocery.

The present lift bridge and frame canal building are bordered by some of the best kept grounds along the state waterway. Once the site was called Podunk. Now the canal has little influence in Holley's life and only when some political spellbinder, seeking votes, comes by canal boat for a rally, does Podunk awake from slumber.

*　　*　　*　　*

Podunk has a special place in the memories of Mr. and Mrs. Egbert R. Cain of Mulberry Street, Rochester. On May 12, 1903 they were married at the bride's home in Holley and after the ceremony, the younger guests flocked to the railroad station to bestow the usual shower of rice and other parting attentions. But the bridal party fooled them by boarding a steam yacht at Podunk for Rochester. It had never been done before, according to the oldest inhabitant.

So the old canal, you see, has been a "honeymoon trail," too.

Holley has also been a favorite spot for firemen's conventions, carnivals, celebrations and sporting events. Pete Esse of West High Terrace in Rochester, now 70, remembers a Fourth of July celebration in Holley at the turn of the century when a bicycle race from Holley to the Ridge was a feature. Esse and some 40 other speed kings of Rochester and vicinity were entered.

It was a blazing hot day and the farmers, along the line, wishing to be helpful, stood beside the route with buckets of water with which they doused the racers. They overdid the attentions. Pete Esse remembers after 45 years what the dousing did to his racing tights.

* * * *

The word vinegar does not ordinarily carry a pleasant connotation. Yet the pungent odor of vinegar wafted over Holley is a pleasant one and moreover, it comes from what the villagers claim is the largest vinegar works in the world.

The industry began at Clarendon, three miles south of Holley, more than a century ago, when the Pettingill brothers, David and T. E., started a combination saw, flour and cider mill to fit all the seasons. Around 1872, Walter S. Pettingill, son of David, and Ogden S. Miller converted the business into a vinegar factory. In 1888, to save the haul to railroad and canal, the plant was moved to Holley. Walter's son, Benjamin M. Pettingill, one of Holley's leading boosters, operated it prior to its sale to the Duffy-Mott interests with which he is now associated.

Holley is set in a rich orchard and vegetable country. Apples and tomatoes are prime crops. The village has a large canning factory. Once the dried apple industry was a considerable one and shipments of dried and barrelled fruits by canal were heavy. Now it's all by rail and truck.

And the only relic of the abandoned interurban line is an old brown R. L. and B. car, standing idle in a farmer's yard, just east of the village.

Many Italians came in the 1870s and 80s to work in the eight or nine stone quarries of the town. After the quarries gave up the ghost, the Latins remained to till the soil and work in the food plants. They are a highly regarded segment of the community. For years their Mount Carmel Society was active in every civic endeavor.

* * * *

The first real old time canaller I met after leaving the tug was Albert Lavendar, who lives on a farm southeast of the village. He is a rugged man in his seventies with vivid recollections of his boating days.

He was born at Shelby Basin on the banks of the canal and as a boy of nine drove mules on his father's boat across the state—at the prevailing wages of $20 per month and keep. Throughout his youth, he worked on the canal in season, turning to the barreling of apples in the fall.

"Fights? Well, it was hard to keep out of them," Lavendar grinned reminiscently. "Generally they happened when boats tried to 'hog the locks' and beat the other fellow through. Smart captains used to have a piece of silver ready for the lock tender. That got results."

Lavendar told how the canal boats sometimes were "frozen in" and had to tie up for the winter wherever the ice trapped them. Once he was caught with a load of grain right in his home town of Holley, "a good break."

He recalled the generally "good grub" on the boats although the crews sometimes tired of too much "Black Rock turkey," which was canalese for salt pork, "streak o' lean and streak o' fat."

* * * *

Who'd think you'd meet in Holley, N. Y., a distinguished English geographer, who is in the British Who's Who and is currently an exchange professor at Bowdoin?

Dr. John Fleur is his name and he has been a professor of geography at Manchester University for some 15 years. He and

Mrs. Fleur were house guests of Mr. and Mrs. Ben Pettingill. The professor has a white Van Dyke beard, he speaks in the precise, deliberate British manner, the horrors of the Nazi blitz have lined his face and all in all, he is a very interesting man.

I fancy Dr. John Fleur of Manchester University felt rather at home in Holley, with its public square, its trim lawns and hedges.

The Holley Standard of Sept. 17, 1870, carried this item:

"Mr. E. D. Olds, host of the Mansion House, has been improving his premises and slicking up generally. Not the least of these improvements is a new sign."

There was no mention of the two young Olds boys that were romping about the Mansion House, now replaced by a modern hotel.

One of them, the late George D. Olds, became president of Amherst to climax a distinguished career as an educator.

The other Olds boy, the versatile Nathaniel S., who will be remembered by old time Rochesterians as a reporter on the Post Express and a historian, went to New York years ago to engage in sales promotion work. For some years under the pen name of the Stroller, he has written a column for the Greenwich Villager.

Greenwich Village seems a far cry from Holley Village, but Columnist Olds only last March lamented bitterly that he could obtain in the metropolis no Northern Spies, "the best of the upstate apples," which were among the fondest recollections of his boyhood in Holley, N. Y.

Thus do memories of his bucolic youth haunt a sophisticate far from the blossom country.

In 1860 a boy was born in a Clarendon farmhouse who became a famous naturalist, big game hunter and taxidermist. Carl Akeley, even as a school boy, was forever mounting birds and one of his early collections some eight years ago, after his death, came to light in the neighborhood and now is housed in New York's Museum of Natural History.

Two other native sons who attained the top rung of the Rochester financial ladder were the late Thomas W. Finucane and the late John N. Beckley.

Maybe Holley, at Orleans' eastern gate, should be annexed by Monroe County. I found the tie that binds the village to the city on the Genesee far stronger than any bond with Albion, the shire town to the westward.

* * * *

Time seems to stand still at the old canal port of Hulberton, between Albion and Holley.

There for a little way the Towpath is just as in the days of yore. There stands an old time canal grocery, a landmark along the Ditch, little changed by the years.

At Hulberton decades slip away and in fancy you see the mules and the horses plodding again along the Towpath. Collars hide terrible shoulder galls on some of them. The drivers spur them on with whip and picturesque profanity. The mules bray, sensing that their six-hour shift is done and it is time to change teams. Drivers grab them, not by their heads, but by their tails and ease them from boat to Towpath to stable. Fresh mules are "tailed" aboard to take their places.

The lines of boats trading at the canal grocery of J. Moore & Sons extend almost as far as the eye can see. Moore's is known all along the Ditch. It sells everything for the canal trade, towlines, pitch for calking boats, horse collars, fish, sugar, brown and white, in barrels, fresh fruit, wood for cook stoves.

Every boat owner has credit at Moore's. They'll pay up at season's end. Moore's loses few accounts. Canallers are honest in the main.

A hay press is in operation at Moore's. The hay, when baled, will be sold, along with oats grown in the countryside, to the boat men. Farmers from miles around trade at Moore's. The quarries are going full blast and there are many stone boats on the Erie.

But that scene lives only in the halls of memory. Only recently the last of the Moores, John C., retired from the business his family had operated so long. A tradition of the old canal has gone.

The canal itself is streamlined and singularly quiet. Hulberton drowses beside the Towpath, dreaming of the brave days of old.

Reapers and Romances

WHEN the canal town was very young, the Indians called it "The Red Village" because there were so many brick houses.

Today red roses bloom on the old Towpath in that "Red Village" which in its 123 years has played no insignificant role in the epic of America.

Somehow I like to think that the murky Erie water flows a little swifter there as if remembering the yesterdays when it bore away to the corners of the earth the products made upon its banks.

But maybe you've always thought Brockport was just an ordinary village?

Possibly you did not know that:

In Brockport were manufactured the first 100 harvesters made in the world.

The first large field of wheat ever harvested by machine was on a farm in the Town of Sweden.

Pioneer bean planters, corn drills, reapers with automatic rakes, grain separators and an amazing array of other implements that eased the lot of the farmer were born of Brockport's inventive genius and productive ability.

Nearly 40 of the best selling novels of the long Victorian age were written in an old fashioned brown house in the village.

Brockport was once called the bean center of America.

Machinery produced in Brockport ended drudgery for thousands; books written in Brockport brought enjoyment to millions.

Has any village of 3,600 contributed more?

* * * *

Twice in recent years the national spotlight that seeks out the unusual has swung on the fruit belt village.

Remember the "White Indian" boys and Richard Marsh, the Brockport explorer who brought them out of the Panama jungles in 1924? And the furor their fair skin and yellow hair caused among scientists who finally labeled them albinos?

Remember the shaggy, black mongrel pup named Idaho that a Brockport youth brought home from a western CCC camp and the drama of 1936 when the dog, accused of drowning a 14-year-old boy swimming in the canal, won his fight for life while the nation watched a court of justice in Brockport's Village Hall?

But you say, Brockport's past may have been both important and colorful. What about its present and future?

Just try to find parking space on its Main Street in this year of 1945.

* * * *

After the canal surveyors had run their stakes south of the Ridge, shrewd pioneers reasoned that wherever the Ditch intersected the Lake Road, running southward from Clarkson, there would be the trading center.

Shrewdest among the pioneers were two New Englanders, Hiel Brockway and James Seymour. They became the most influential of Brockport's founders. They also became bitter rivals.

Seymour had settled in Clarkson and did his utmost to get that then thriving Ridge Road center on the Canal. He did succeed in swinging the waterway some distance to the north. No other Ridge Road village is so near the Canal as Clarkson. The route of the Ditch describes a considerable curve to reach Brockport, thanks to James Seymour.

Seymour bought land on the east side of the Lake Road, now Brockport's Main Street. Brockway bought on the west side. And thereby hangs a tale.

"East is east and west is west and never the twain shall meet." And Seymour streets on the east never meet Brockway streets on the west—with two exceptions, State and Erie. None of the others intersecting Main Street downtown join. That zigzag street layout is a reminder of an old feud between two strong men.

In 1823 Brockport became the temporary western terminus of the Canal, instead of Rochester as first planned. The founders of Brockport saw to that.

Swiftly the Red Village rose beside the newly dug channel. The bricks that went into the stores and dwellings came from a bed north of Clarkson.

The settlement was named in honor of Hiel Brockway, who became the village magnate with his busy boat yard and his ownership of the Red Jacket packet line. His great-great grandson, Lamonte Brockway, Rochester insurance and real estate man, told me that the village was first called Brockwayport, a name that was almost immediately shortened to Brockport.

Not so many years ago, cannon balls were found imbedded in old trees in Quackenbush's woods near the Canal. Some people figured a battle had been fought there, perhaps in the War of 1812. Historians deduced they were fired from the guns that lined the canal banks for the salute to the Clinton flotilla that opened the Ditch in 1825.

From its inception, Brockport in the town of Sweden has been the most important community in Monroe County west of the Genesee River. No one seems to know how the town came to be named Sweden. There is no record of a Swedish settlement.

In the early days business and industry centered around the canal. Throngs jammed the high bridge when Lafayette rode the waterway on his tour of 1825.

For many years until the tolls were abolished, all boats stopped at Brockport, for there was the office of the collector. The old toll office, back of the Dunn Block along the Heelpath, was torn down only a few years ago.

*　　　*　　　*　　　*

In 1844 a young West Virginia inventor, a former blacksmith, came riding into Brockport on horseback. His name was Cyrus McCormick. Thirteen years before he had invented a clumsy device for harvesting wheat. He spent years in Washington getting his patent and improving his machine that would do the work of seven men with cradles. He sought a factory that would make his reapers. In Washington he met Congressman E. B. Holmes of Brockport. Holmes told him about the Bacchus and Burroughs iron works in his home town which had been making farm tools since 1828.

McCormick gave the Brockport works an order to make 100 harvesters. They were unsatisfactory although one of them, taken to the Sweden farm of Frederick Root, is said to have harvested the first field of wheat ever cut by machinery in America.

But Brockport had another iron works, newly established, that took over McCormick's order. So it came about that in 1846 in a small shop beside the Canal, William H. Seymour and Dayton S. Morgan produced for Cyrus McCormick the first successful harvesters, 100 of them, the world had ever known.

One of those machines today is in the Henry Ford Muesum.

McCormick moved on to Chicago and millions. From Brockport poured a steady flow of inventions that revolutionized the farm implement industry.

Farmer Root, whose grain had been harvested by the pioneer reaper, perfected a grain separator and cleaner. Seymour brought out for the harvest of 1851 the automatic raking reaper, "The Quadrant Platform," that has never since been materially altered; D. S. Morgan made and shipped to far corners of the world his Triumph reapers for 20 years. There were also the Gordon automatic grain binder and plow; the Johnson harvester; the corn drill, devised by Whiteside, Barnett & Allen; the first bean planter, invented by William Bradford.

D. S. Morgan made reapers until 1894. The next year flames devoured the plant. The huge Johnson Harvester factory succeeded the old Bacchus and Burroughs foundry and made thousands of machines beside the Canal from 1868 to 1882 when the plant burned down and was moved to Batavia. The year of the fire Johnson's had made 6,000 machines and at its peak employed 400 to 500 hands.

Well into the 1890s Brockport was a world center of farm machinery production. Disastrous fires, changing times and the development of the Western wheat fields ended her supremacy in that field.

* * * *

But Brockport went on making a remarkable variety of other things—the Ultra shoe, the Capen piano, the Gleason cooling board, a necessary adjunct for the embalmer. The Wheel Works made racing sulkeys with tubular frames. A. D. Daly evolved a combination footstool and cuspidor.

In the 1880s more beans were shipped from Brockport than any other point in America. There were huge warehouses in the village before that industry moved westward as had the others.

Today Brockport industry is centered around canning and cold storage plants. She shares in the new frozen food boom. A huge A&P cannery sprawls over many acres on the eastern end of the village and the frozen food plant recently absorbed the old Monroe County fair grounds. Hundreds live in Brockport and work in Rochester.

* * * *

During the years the Red Village was turning out reapers, pianos, shoes and cooling boards, a slim, well groomed, bewigged lady in a brown house in shady College Street was turning out best selling novels—38 of them in 50 years.

Mary Jane Holmes was the novelist's name. It is a name that will awaken memories for most of us over 50. The others probably never heard of her. But in her time she had the biggest following for the longest time of any American author. Sales of her books topped the two million mark.

My grandmother doted on the saccharine, conventionally melodramatic love stories that flowed from the pen of Mary Jane Holmes —and so did yours. Lena Rivers, English Orphans, The Homestead on the Hillside, Meadowbrook, Bad Hugh—they passed from hand to hand in rural villages, in rough mining towns and in fashionable drawing rooms—from the Civil War past the turn of the century and the dawn of a new age in America. With that new age of movies, jazz, divorce, speed and noisy, smelly automobiles, Mary Jane Holmes, a pious Victorian lady, writing sweet unrealities in a quiet village, could have no part.

New England, born Mary Jane and her frail lawyer-husband, Daniel Holmes, came to live in the canal town in 1853. The author had already produced Tempest and Sunshine and was on the road to literary glory. New York magazines were running her stories in serial form.

She amassed no great fortune. She made enough to live comfortably; to travel abroad a great deal and to accumulate a large collection of curios from all corners of the globe.

Mrs. Holmes was active in village good works and the WCTU. She taught a Sunday School class. She never wrote a line that would offend the most·puritannical.

She was pretty strait laced but she was warmly human, too. Brockport youngsters who got cookies and other goodies from the lady in the Brown Cottage knew that. She used some of their first names in her books although she placed all of the scenes of her romances in New England, the South or in Europe, never in Western New York where she lived most of her 79 years.

Mary Jane came back to the Brown Cottage to die in 1907 after a visit to her girlhood home in Massachusetts. Her funeral was the biggest Brockport ever knew. Messages came from all over the world. Metropolitan editors commented on the passing of one of America's most prolific and popular writers. Grandma, thumbing her well worn copy of Cousin Maude, could not believe that Mary Jane Holmes was no more.

* * * *

Old residents will tell you how when the crowing of roosters disturbed her writing, Mrs. Holmes bought up every bird in the neighborhood.

Her wisp-like husband followed her in death within 12 years. Daniel Holmes was subject to intermittent sieges of malaria. Sometimes he had to be carried up the two flights of stairs to his office. The Baptist ladies had a chair placed on the church lawn so that he might stop there and rest.

The Brown Cottage, after his death, was divided and remodeled beyond recognition.

Mrs. Holmes' writing followed the pattern of the times. Her heroes were handsome and brave, her heroines paragons of virtue;

her villains incredibly wicked and always there was the happy ending. Here is a sample of her literary style, from Lena Rivers, the story that has been enacted by thousands of "home talent" thespians and a few years ago was made into a movie:

"But at last, as days glided into weeks and weeks into months, hope died away and when the days grew bright and gladsome in the warm spring sun and when the snow melted on the mountain top and the first robin's note was heard at the farmhouse door, Helena laid her baby on her mother's bosom and without a murmur, glided down the darkening river whose deep waters move onward, ever onward, but never return."

A brutally realistic rewrite man would boil that 75-word sentence down into the simple statement that:

"Helena died in childbirth in the spring."

But our grandmothers liked Mary Jane's style better.

* * * *

For 113 years Brockport has been a college town.

In 1832 the Baptist Association of Western New York began raising funds for a Collegiate Institute. Hiel Brockway, father of the village, gave six acres of land southeast of the town and $3,000 in cash, with the stipulation that village children could always be educated there. Building began in 1834. But times were hard and the work dragged. Spiders began to weave their webs in the unfinished college.

In 1841 the citizens of Brockport bought the plant for $3,800 and founded a new Institute. On a Sunday in 1854 it burned down while the village was at church. It was rebuilt the next year. In 1867 it was turned over to the state for a Normal School after Brockport had outbid Geneseo and outmaneuvered the powerful Wadsworths.

Only recently the name was changed to the State Teachers'

College and in 1939 a massive $1,100,000 red brick Georgian building supplanted the old Normal, where so many schoolma'ams and masters had been trained.

The College is planning further expansion. A score of houses bordering the campus are to be torn down to make way for a pretentious dormitory program.

In this year of war, men are virtually non existent at the Teachers' College. But the girls are everywhere, on the streets, in the ice cream parlors, in the buses, to add charm and vivacity to the many-sided Brockport scene.

* * * *

Many of Brockport's citizens have been important. Others have been only colorful.

"Calico Jack" belongs in the latter category. She was born Emma Hunt. Her mother, Elizabeth Tripp Hunt, in 1860, started building "Hunt's Castle" on the Colby Road in East Sweden. After $20,000 had been put into the structure, with its 12 rooms, some of them 17 feet high and all with black walnut woodwork, and including two elaborate ball rooms, the funds gave out. So there were no front steps to "The Castle."

But it had a cupola and from there "Calico Jack," after her mother's demise, would spy on the field hands with a telescope.

No community knew a more bizarre character. She would ride to town on a cream-colored horse. She wore a costly sealskin coat. She smoked cigars and, according to legend, would light them with dollar bills.

After she went broke and the "Castle" was sold at sheriff's sale, "Calico Jack" moved to Rochester. Her last job was that of charwoman at the Central Station. The "Castle" is just a farm residence now.

* * * *

Horatio M. Beach, publisher and diplomat, in 1856 founded the weekly Republic, which survives today as the merged Republic-Democrat. The present operators have the surname, Blossom, an appropriate one in a land of orchards. P. A. Blossom has been the publisher since 1899. His son, E. M., is business manager.

Around 1880 Beach returned from a consular post in Germany and brought back what was hailed as the first internal combustion engine in America. Set up in the Republic office to power the machinery there, it was a monstrous thing with a flywheel weighing half a ton. It used illuminating gas for fuel. But it could generate only 3 horsepower!

* * * *

The Soldiers Memorial Tower, now a crumbling ruin in a desolate field, was a brain child of the same Horatio Beach. In 1882 he led a movement for a cemetery, centering around a plot for veterans of the Civil War. An iron railing was built around the field, some burials were made, a vault and a chapel were constructed.

In 1894 work began on the tower. It is 60 feet high, of Medina sandstone, with a battlement effect at its crest. Inside was a circular iron stairway that thousands have climbed to obtain a superb view of the countryside. At one time the New York Central Railroad listed the memorial as one of the scenic attractions along its route.

After Beach's death the cemetery enterprise waned. The remains were removed to other burying grounds, until only three graves, those of soldiers without known kin, were left. They are still there and every Memorial Day, the American Legion decks them with flags.

The vault has been razed and the chapel burned down. The tower is crumbling and massive stones have slipped down from the battlement. The circular stairway is rusting away. It is the most unusual war memorial I have ever seen.

When I was traveling the Long Level by canal tug boat, the captain pointed to the tower in the distance and said: "We have been wondering for years what that is—a monument, the chimney of a burned building, a smoke stack or what?"

I told him I'd find out. Well, Captain Tom, here's your answer.

*   *   *   *

George Guelf is no ordinary villager. He is a naturalist who knows every tree, bush and bird of the region. A kindly, observant philosopher, he has lived all his long life in Brockport.

Ray Tuttle, a much younger man, is a sort of unofficial village historian. For years he has been collecting the lore of the community. Ray took George and me on a tour, pointing out interesting and historic spots. It was old stuff to George and highly fascinating to me.

From George's memories, Ray's scrap book, my own observations and other sources, I caught these random, kaleidoscopic pictures of life in the canal town:

Rafts laden with logs floating down the lakes and the canal all the way from Michigan in the 1880's to the Gordon saw mill . . . the old lift bridge manipulated by a series of weights . . . the tallyho from the Gordon stables . . . the bustle around the canal banks in the 80's and 90's, with the shoe factory by the high bridge, the harvester works, the Morgan reaper plant, the grain warehouses, the toll office, the 4,000-foot "railroad" from the Heelpath to the harvester works, with its flat car pulled by horses. . . . The tomb stone in High Street Cemetery of Joseph Roby which tells that he was a participant in the famous Boston Tea Party of Dec. 16, 1773 and later a captain in the Revolution.

The Rising Sun district school, east of the village, so named because it faces the east and retaining its old title despite any slogan of the Nipponese . . . houses along the Towpath where now the roses grow . . . the old mule cemetery . . . the old county fairgrounds and George recalling how as a boy he helped clear pebbles from the race tracks that were to know so many flying hooves . . . huge drays hauling the mail from Moore's nationally known magazine agency . . . the old American Hotel, a relic of canal days with traces of old doorways at the level of the Clinton Ditch . . . it's the Hotel Brockport now but the old name is still sprawled across its front under the roof. . . .

Ward's Opera House, that burned in 1911, and Al Fields and the "Tom" shows and East Lynne and the show bands that serenaded the hands at the harvester and reaper works . . . the Winslow Music Hall and the RL&B trolleys clattering by . . . Old Home Week in 1911. . . . The steam freight packets, the Frankie Reynolds, the John Owens and the others at the busy docks. . . .

The big house where the politically potent Dailey boys, John F., Don, Vince and Murray among them, were born and the barley-laden wagons lined up for a quarter of a mile before the Dailey warehouses 35 years ago—the influence of the old families, notably the Morgans and the Gordons, extending beyond Brockport limits (Buffalo has a D. S. Morgan Building)—John Pallace, colorful politico and collector of the port, commuting between his Brockport home and his city office—the Garden Club planting a quarter mile of rose bushes along the old Towpath—the dog, Idaho, freed from "prison" and dying under the wheels of a car.—The war days, the LSTs and the PT boats and the sub chasers gliding along Erie water, bound for battle on the seas—Elsie Blossom's painting of picturesque Water Street—the old and the new mingled in the port that the Indians called the Red Village so long ago.

Cradle of the Stars

BORN—In the year 1825, of New England parentage and suckled by the Clinton Ditch, on the farm of Daniel Spencer in the town of Ogden, the port called Spencer's Basin.

But when people got to calling the place simply "The Basin," the village fathers renamed it Spencerport. There were already too many "basins" on the canal. Besides the new name was more seemly for a port of growing importance—and it was more dignified.

Seemliness and dignity belong to New England and the New England strain is strong in the Ogden blood. It was put there 143 years ago when Ogden Town was Fairfield, long before there was a canal or any ports or basins; when the first settlers from New England put to the plow the land in which still live so many of their descendants, Spencers among them.

The pretty village at Rochester's western gate has certain New Englandish physical characteristics, too. The visitor notes the snug, unpretentious, homelike homes, so many of them painted white, under giant elms; the thin white spire—that of a Congregational Church, again in the New England tradition—reaching skyward above the town; the preponderance of Anglo-Saxon residents; the absence either of excessive wealth or extreme poverty; the tranquility of the main street with its chairs where old men may sit in the sun. The hasty observer is likely to add up all these things and get "New England."

But Spencerport is not New England. She is Western New York. Above all she is herself.

Because only 10 miles separate the residential village and the industrial city and because so many people work in Rochester and sleep in Spencerport, some might say "Oh, another suburb."

Again, they are wrong. Spencerport is not "another suburb." She is Spencerport, serene, decorous, ever charming and with a proper New Englandish dignity.

* * * *

The town hall at East Haddam, Conn. was crowded for the "Genesee meeting." James Wadsworth spoke with fire and feeling of the possibilities for settlers in the Genesee Country. True, he had land to sell—at $2 an acre, but more than that, he had a vision of a fertile and prosperous countryside where all was wilderness. The year was 1802.

In the audience was young George Willey. Soon he was on his way to the Genesee Country afoot, his ax slung over his shoulder. He was the first settler to rear a cabin in the town that was to bear the name of William Ogden of New York, an early land speculator. For that he received a prize offered by Wadsworth.

Let a native-born poetess, Mrs. Augusta E. Nichols-Rich, reading the centennial ode at Ogden's 100th anniversary celebration in 1902, go on with the tale of the award:

> "—— It was simply this:
> Of wheat six bushels, one barrel of pork,
> And one of whisky, which was freely shared
> With all; yea! that they lose no time going
> Round the barrel, it was tapped at either
> End, and little drink remained when the last
> Log was fitted into place."

For a conservative sort of town, Ogden had a lusty beginning.

Other pioneers came from New England, the four tall Colby brothers, the Websters, the three Spencers, William H., Daniel and Austin; the Nicholses, the Hills, the Trues and many more whose descendants still live in the neighborhood.

Ogden Center became the principal settlement and James Wadsworth had great hopes for it. Only recently has the last Wadsworth land in Ogden passed out of the hands of the Valley dynasty. West of the Center another hamlet was founded with the curious name of Ogden Town Pump because of the pump that stood for many years at the intersection of the highways.

The star of Ogden Center waned as the Ditch pushed through Spencer's farm and lots were sold for the village, that soon became a shipping point for lumber, grain, and fruit and was known far and wide as "The Basin."

A cultural child of the old Center still survives in the Ogden Farmers' Library now housed in the Spencerport Village Building. It was founded in a store in 1815 and only three free libraries in the state are older—and one of them is the Farmers Library of Garbutt, born in 1805.

By 1876 the Ogden Library was dormant and so it remained until 1908, when, under the leadership of the late Supreme Court Justice George A. Benton, one of Spencerport's most distinguished and influential men, it was reorganized and moved to the canal village. The old books, 141 of them, were collected from scattered homes and one can see them today in the village library. One book plate bears the date of 1799.

James Wadsworth deeded to the association two acres of land with the stipulation that it could never be sold. So today the library has on its hands some real estate for which it has scant use.

* * * *

In the Farmers' Library is a framed picture of an old gentleman with luxuriant whiskers. It might be Longfellow or Whittier. It is one of their literary contemporaries, John Townsend Trowbridge. He was born in a log house in Nichols Street in 1827. His name is hardly remembered now but he wrote 50 volumes that were best sellers in their time.

Trowbridge's "Neighbor Jackwood," his most popular work, written in 1857, was one of the first realistic novels of New England life. He also wrote "Cudjo's Cave," depicting the thrilling adventures of a runaway slave; the Jack Hazard series, the Tide Mill series, all prized by young readers who devoured them by candlelight.

Trowbridge was a poet, too. His first verse was published in a Rochester newspaper when he was 17. His most famous verse, "Darius Green and His Flying Machine," is said to have been based upon the experiments in aviation of an unidentified Ogden neighbor.

The author, when 27 years old, went to New York and later to Arlington, Mass., where he died at the age of 88. At the time of the Ogden Centennial in 1902, he paid this tribute to the old library in a letter:

"For me it held infinite riches, for there were the great Waverly novels, the Leather Stocking tales of Cooper, Shakespeare, Byron, Plutarch, Hume and the Spectator—history, poetry, romance."

Today an historical marker stands before the house in Nichols Street where a distinguished American man of letters lived as a boy.

Some years ago, on motion of the scholarly Ernest R. Clark, then a resident of Spencerport, the village school was renamed the John T. Trowbridge School. But somehow the name never stuck. But then, Ernest R. Clark has led many other lost causes.

*   *   *   *

Now after many years another Spencerport youth is following the Trowbridge tradition. William Kehoe is only 22; he was grad-

When They "Tailed 'Em" Aboard

Excursion Days of the Gay 90's at Spencerport

uated from the village high school in 1940 and won the Avery Hopwood prize for literature while a student at the University of Michigan. His first novel, "Sweep of Dust" is out and his mother, Mrs. Mable Kehoe, who lives in Spencerport, and all the neighbors are proud of Bill and you see "Sweep of Dust" on many a village table.

* * * *

The Congregational Church is really a bit of New England—pearly white with an old fashioned stone basement with side door and a generous sweep of lawn, its spire dominating the village scene.

In 1850 it broke off, amid some acrimony, from the Ogden Presbyterian Church. The founders of the new parish vowed to have a spire higher than the mother church. The new edifice, dedicated in February, 1852, fulfilled the pledge. The building burned down in November of the same year but the doughty flock soon rebuilt it, with a spire higher than the first one.

The first minister was the Rev. James Morton Dill. During his pastorate, in 1854, a son, who was christened James Brooks Dill, arrived at the parsonage. This boy went to New York and was one of the most successful corporation lawyers of America.

The boy who was born in a Spencerport parsonage performed superservice for the big corporations. He is said to have been the first lawyer ever to receive a million dollar fee. That was for weaving together the intricate fabric of the Steel Trust. Mark Sullivan, in "Our Times," suggests that Dill was the father of the law that has made New Jersey such a snug haven for giant corporations.

Dill died in 1910 but not before he had given a memorial window to the church where his father preached and had made a trip back to his birthplace to deliver an address. No one recalls what he said on that occasion but Sullivan in his book states that Dill once began a Harvard lecture with the proud declaration that "I am the lawyer for a billion dollars of invested capital."

* * * *

So much for the minister's son. Now for a minister's daughter who once called Spencerport home. Around 1910 the Methodist Conference assigned the Rev. Peter Thompson to the Spencerport church. The Rev. Peter, a smallish man, with a good singing voice, had a second wife, two daughters and a son. The younger daughter, Margaret, and the son Peter Jr., attended the local school. The older daughter attended high school at Hamburg, their former home, and later, Syracuse University. She was in Spencerport only at vacation time during her father's five-year pastorate. Her name was Dorothy. Yes, she was THE Dorothy Thompson.

Mrs. Florence Ring, who as a girl lived across the street from the Thompsons and who sang with Dorothy in the church choir, remembers the teen age Thompson daughter as "full of pep, smart and witty. She was slender, not very tall, with brown hair and blue eyes." She sang alto in the choir.

And once when the Rev. Peter was ill, Dorothy Thompson, home from college, preached in his stead. The congregation of the Spencerport Methodist Church thus was one of the first audiences of the many that this famous woman has addressed.

* * * *

In the early days of the century, a tow headed girl lived in a humble home in Spencerport. Her name was Clara Luce. Later on Clara became Clair. She went to the village school and in vacations picked fruit in nearby orchards. She had a blond beauty; she was shapely; she loved to dance and above all, she had a flaming ambition.

So she came to Rochester to work in Eastman Kodak dark rooms to earn money for dancing lessons. She worked as a cigaret girl in a downtown restaurant. A Rochester dancing teacher, Florence Colebrook Powers, took the girl under her wing and after that Clair Luce's rise was rapid—but always marked by hard work and study of her art.

Her dancing feet carried her to Broadway and the Follies in 1927. She had a fling at the movies and the spoken stage; she married a millionaire and divorced him; she went to Europe, took London by storm and danced with Fred Astaire before King Edward VIII. She stayed in London during the blitz, giving shows for soldiers. Her name is known on two continents.

And that's the glamorous career of the tow headed girl who once lived "on the wrong side of the tracks" in Spencerport, N. Y.

* * * *

A few months ago a Spencerport High School alumnus, Eugene C. Auchter, whose mother lives in Elm Grove Road, was mentioned as the next Secretary of Agriculture. He did not get that job but Auchter, regarded as a foremost agricultural scientist, has recently taken over the directorship of Pine Apple Research in Hawaii. Edward Amish, now of Rochester, recalls how he and Gene Auchter used to skate from Spencerport to Elm Grove and back on the frozen Erie Canal.

* * * *

So Spencerport has been, in a sense, "the cradle of the stars." Few villages her size can boast so many boys and girls "who made good" in such varied fields as literature, journalism, finance, agriculture and the stage.

* * * *

Approaching the village by canal boat, one is impressed by the seeming antiquity of the town. On either side of the lift bridge are two weather beaten frame buildings that look as old as the Ditch itself.

One of them is. The building with the cupola on the south corner has been a store since 1826.

The other, now the home of the Weekly Star, once was a grain warehouse and its shape fits the contours of the canal. It was built in 1876 after the fire that swept the whole side of the street.

Before the lift bridge, there was the "High Bridge." Then the farm wagons had to climb steep inclines and the "waterfront" scene was a busier one. The dock back of the Star building was laden with barrels of apples and potatoes and other produce.

The pioneer "Produce King" was James Upton. Soon after the Canal was built, two young men and their brides came riding westward on the ditch from Albany. One was Upton. The other was his chum, Leland Stanford. The Uptons got off at Spencerport. The Stanfords went on West to eventual riches and power. But James Upton played no insignificant role in his smaller sphere.

He built the mansion on the West Ridge that is now the home of the Ridgemont Country Club, which, according to his grandson, Charles A. Pomeroy, contained the first bath room in Monroe County. Upton began extensive growing and shipping of fruit and other produce, with Spencer's Basin his major port. After James Upton's death, his widow and family went to Spencerport to live. There the seven Upton sons grew up and made their impress on the community. Witness the Upton Building, the Upton Block, the one-time Upton Hotel and Upton Fire Department. All the sons, save Charles Stanford, the originator of the famous Rochester lamp, carried on their father's produce business.

*   *   *   *

Beside the lift bridge where the 83-year-old flagman, Joe Plucknett, keeps the state grounds so neat and well shrubbed, were once the canal hotels: The Palmer, later Tom Tunney's, and on the west end, Johnny Leonard's. Leonard, when Ogden went dry, opened the "Red Onion" just over the line in the town of Greece. On Union Street, where the Matheos ice cream plant now stands, was the three-story, white Lincoln House, once the Upton, and a well known hostelry in its day. It was razed some 20 years ago.

In the early 1900's the Rochester, Lockport and Buffalo electric line and the Barge Canal were being built at the same time. Workers on those projects, plus the floating fruit pickers and the canallers, brought some lively times to the ordinary staid village.

Spencerport never was much of an industrial town. In the early days she had a blast furnace and a tannery. Later on there was a cannery and for many years the Hoy potato digger was made in the village. Before the Barge Canal was built, a slip ran from the old waterway north of the buildings on Union Street.

And there was—and is—the fireworks industry. Judge Benton once operated a fireworks factory along the canal. Eight years ago Amerigo Antonelli, Rochester "Fireworks King" and the son of the royal pyrotechnician to the King of Italy, began making fireworks in the sheds that dot the canal bank at the eastern end of the village. When the war came, he obtained large government contracts for bombs and grenades.

The arrest of Antonelli and some of his aides on charges of making defective bombs, their trials and convictions, followed by the passing of the plant into other and more reputable hands—that is recent history. Spencerporters prefer not to talk about it.

* * * *

And here are some stray fragments from the village's past and present:

The cable that stood for years in the bed of the old canal, a memento of the failure in the 1880s of the Belgian cable steam towing experiment between Buffalo and Rochester—the Malay brothers, Corydon and the younger Leroy, editing the Star as did their father before them, watching the village scene through the years and in later days the dwindling canal traffic from the windows of their plant that was once a grain warehouse—the glory of Spencerport as the greatest of cabbage shipping centers, around 1890. The shipments were by rail—Ernest R. Clark's boyhood memories of the old mill pond—Sig Sautelle's and other circuses coming to town by canal boat and the smaller shows that held forth on board ship—the state scow that David B. Hill Democrats in 1893 loaded with canal workers and floaters to turn the tide in Adams Basin caucus—the eternal rivalry in sports between Spencerport and Hilton—the dead whale that went on tour via canal boat and stank to the heavens—the schoolboy Cadets organized by Judge Benton—the lush days of the interurbans when 315 tickets to Rochester were sold in a single day—all these and many more memories, grave and gay, cluster around the town that began as a "basin" and ended as a "port."

* * * *

In 1802 a pioneer physician, Dr. John Webster, of Massachusetts bought land where now the Trimmer Road crosses the canal. When a small pox epidemic raged along the waterway, he set up a hospital along the banks of the Ditch. One of his patients was a traveling evangelist, the Rev. Isaac Fister. On his recovery, the minister settled the doctor's bill by preaching for months without pay in Adams Basin Methodist Church. Later he became the regular pastor.

The doctor's son, Alvin, worked the farm after his father's death. A rabid Abolitionist, he maintained a station of the Underground Railway there. His son, the late Judson H., ran the farm for some years and during the winter, boarded the canal horses and mules, sometimes as many as 75 head. The place became known as Webster's Basin.

For nearly a decade after 1892, Judson Webster was one of the operators of the Buffalo and Rochester Transit Company which ran steam freight packets on the Canal.

A grove near Webster's Basin was the scene of many boat excursions from Rochester, sedate Sunday school picnics as well as gayer Elks parties. The William B. Kirk was the best known excursion boat.

Three miles west of Spencerport is Adams Basin, born of the

Clinton Ditch, now a quiet hamlet with only the ruins of old warehouses to tell of the days when it was a considerable port.

First it bore the cumbersome name of Adams' and King's Basin, from two sets of brothers who founded it: Marcus, Abner and Myron Adams and Moses and Bradford King. They established stores, warehouses, saw mills. In its day Adams Basin shipped a lot of produce.

Marcus Adams in his memoirs recalls that the port was famous along the Ditch because of its shrewd horse traders who unloaded broken-down animals on the boatmen.

Abner Adams had the contract for digging the Ditch in the Adams Basin sector. He was the great-grandfather of Samuel Hopkins Adams, of Auburn, distinguished author of "Revelry," "Incredible Era" and of "Canal Town." The last named book is dedicated to his ancestor.

In the 1880's the saw mill of Joel Milliner was a busy place. Logs from the Canadian forests were rafted down from Tonawanda with sometimes a single horse pulling six sections of logs hitched together. The logs were rolled off the Towpath into the nearby mill pond to be sawed by the Milliner mill.

United States Marshal Frank C. Blackford, now a Spencerport resident, was born at Adams Basin and his father, Joseph Blackford, conducted a store and large warehouse there. The marshal's blue eyes glisten as he talks about old canal days, of the old hotel and the cobbler, Pat McNarama, who told a wide eyed young Frank to get his shovel ready for "a boatload of pennies is coming on the canal." The marshal recalled swimming in the Ditch and sometimes encountering dead horses floating down stream. He told of the old waste weirs and how sometimes they went out, flooding the lands.

*   *   *   *

Where the Manitou Road crosses the canal, in the shadow of

the high road embankment, is a lovely old brick Colonial house, full of antique furniture, that was built in 1825 by James Cromwell of New York. His grandson, Frank, lives there today.

First the Ditch cut across the Cromwell land, then the railroad and finally the trolleys. Across the canal from the house on the towpath, long ago stood the Nine Mile Grocery, nine miles from Rochester.

The Cromwells have seen the narrow boats and the mules and the horses and now the wider Ditch and the modern barges. At night their powerful searchlights flood the Cromwell grounds and the sylvan shores and the scene is a picturesque one. By day the view from the historic house so near the Erie water is equally fine. There is natural beauty along any waterway, even the man-made Barge Canal.

A mile to the east is Elm Grove, once South Greece and nicknamed "Henpeck." Once there were warehouses, two canal groceries and a blacksmith shop where canal mules and horses were shod. The "Eight Mile groceries" were operated by Mrs. Hawthorne and by John Service, Frank Cromwell recalled. Now a pleasant suburban community has grown up around the old port of "Henpeck."

*   *   *   *

You may recall that when I rode the Long Level westward by tug in May, I told of a white house near South Greece where the canal men for years had waved to a boy and girl who lived there, had tossed them magazines and the comics, without ever learning their names.

The other day I received a letter which said:

"My brother and I are the boy and girl that the captain and co-pilot of the Matton 21 told you about. My brother is working and I will be a senior at Nazareth Academy next fall. Then I hope to go to college.

Plymouth Ave. Lift Bridge, Rochester

When Rochester's City Hall Was on Towpath

"We want you to know we have enjoyed watching and waving at the boats. We have done it ever since I can remember and we haven't forgotten about the comics and magazines, either.

"I am enclosing a letter to the captain and co-pilot. Would you please forward it to them?"

The letter was signed "Norma Amesbury."

* * * *

Norma, I sent your letter on and I am sure Captain Tom and Poley Miner were delighted to get it.

And it is heart warming to know that in this modern day, the old comradeship between the boatmen and the folks on the shore has not entirely departed.

"Young Lion of the West"

IT was a broad river and power-packed waterfalls that gave Rochester being.

But it was a narrow shallow ditch that made it great.

In her youth, Rochester incurred a debt to the Erie Canal she can never repay.

The canal pumped the life blood of commerce into the heart of a raw settlement in the mud of the river flats and transformed it almost overnight into the boom town of America, the roaring "Young Lion of the West."

The tumbling waters turned the mill wheels but the slow, steady flow of the Clinton Ditch carried the Genesee flour to the markets of the world—and made the city great.

There came a time, after many years, when Rochester, grown rich and powerful, tired of the old waterway that had nurtured the mill town in its youth, that had served so faithfully through the years of maturity. The lift bridges, attuned to the leisurely pace of the canal boats, impeded the swelling flow of downtown motor traffic in the new age of speed. Mules plodding along the Towpath past the very doors of the City Hall—what place had they in the heart of a modern city in the 20th Century?

So the mules and the Towpath were banished forever and the Erie water that had wound through the city for nearly a century, was diverted into a wider, machine-dominated, less picturesque channel on the city's southern rim.

Today whining, roaring subway trains rush through the bed of the old Ditch where once the boats crawled and the mules brayed and the drivers sang and swore.

The remnants of a few old stone locks; the staunch masonry of the second Aqueduct, still in the service of the city after nearly a century; a few old buildings inseparably linked with Towpath days —they are about all the tangible remains of the old canal in Rochester.

But the intangible things, the boyhood memories, such as skating on the Aqueduct rink in winter, diving from "the hoggie bridge" at the Western Widewaters in summer—the very mention of the old canal calls them up out of Never Again Land.

There will remain always the debt Rochester can never pay and the history that the Ditch has written into the annals of the city it built out of the swamps.

*   *   *   *

Shortly before his death in 1828, De Witt Clinton, commenting on the phenomenal growth of Rochester, then with a population of 8,000, recalled that when he passed the Genesee River with other commissioners exploring the route of the Erie Canal only 18 years before, "there was not a house where Rochester now stands."

In 1812 there were two dwellings on the 100-acre tract that the millsite conscious Marylanders, Rochester, Carroll and Fitzhugh, had bought. The population was recorded as 15 souls. But destiny, in the form of Surveyor Geddes' stakes, had marked the falls town as her own. Geddes from the first decided where the canal should cross the Genesee. A later survey, by another surveyor, placed the route 12 miles to the south, Colonel Rochester and his fellow townsmen fought that move down, and Geddes' stakes stood.

By 1815, Rochesterville's populace had grown to 331, the Red Mill had been built and was grinding Genesee wheat and the canal seemed assured. The Young Lion cub was beginning to purr.

Four years later when the route of the Ditch was definitely determined, there were more than 1,200 people living in Rochester, which had at least four flour mills. The next year the census figures were 1,500 and the contract had been awarded for the Rochester section of the canal. I am quoting the census statistics to illustrate the progress of the community as the canal became a reality.

The year of 1822 made canal history. The waterway had been completed westward to the Genesee and on October 29, the first boat laden with Rochester flour left Hill's Basin at the east side of the river for Little Falls. Rochester (the ville had been dropped) housed 4,274 people, 400 of them employed on public works, namely the Aqueduct.

"The Young Lion of the West," was roaring.

*   *   *   *

Ten days after the opening of canal navigation in 1823 (the western section was not complete)—10,000 barrels of flour had been shipped out of Rochester. Nathaniel Rochester, going to market, basket on arm, to Buffalo Street from his Third Ward home, was meeting more and more people he did not know. Everywhere buildings were going up. The bang of the hammer, the rasp of the saw vied with the music of the falls and the grinding mill wheels. Hundreds were crossing the bridge over the river daily, the bridge at which lawmakers scoffed in 1810, asking "Who would use it, muskrats?"

That year saw the completion of the Aqueduct that was to carry the Grand Canal across the Genesee. It was the longest stone arch bridge structure in America. It was the engineering wonder of the world. It was 804 feet long with nine Roman arches. Its walls were of the red Medina sandstone obtained from the river gorge near Carthage, the rival village whose star was setting. Its coping was of gray limestone. The whole work was thoroughly grouted, with massive iron bolts holding the masonry together. And it cost some $87,000.

Two years went into its building, with 30 convicts from Auburn Prison among its builders. One day at the end of work when the prisoners were supposed to march back to their barracks on the island now occupied by City Hall Annex, they tried to stampede the guards and escape. The plot failed. Only a half dozen escaped and all but two or three of them were rounded up in short order.

The first Aqueduct pier was carried away by river torrents and during the spring of 1823 heavy rains and snowstorms hampered the work. But at last the great engineering work was complete and the voice of the Young Lion sounded throughout the land.

But that first Aqueduct was found to leak badly. Besides it allowed passage of only one boat at a time. The result was fights between crews for right of way and consequent delays to the traffic of the Ditch. In 19 years it was replaced by a new structure.

*   *   *   *

A warm sun shone that June 7 of 1825. Evergreen arches hung over the streets, flags waved from buildings, children wore gay scarves and badges. Nearly 10,000 congregated at the basin west of Exchange Street.

A packet boat hove into view. Bells rang, drums rolled and cannon boomed. From the deck of the boat a thin-faced old man waved, smiling at the crowds. Marie Joseph Paul Arthur Gilbert Molier, Marquis de Lafayette, had come to Rochester on his grand tour.

There were dinners and speeches and all traffic on the canal was suspended for the day. Veterans of the Revolution shook hands with their aging general at Hoard's Tavern in Exchange

Street. A tablet in the wall of the Lincoln Bank branch office today marks the site of that reception of 120 years ago.

*   *   *   *

October 26 and 27 of that same year were red leter days, too. On the morning of the 26th men stood in the rain beside cannon lined upon the canal bank, tensely waiting, as if for an invader.

At 10:20 the silence was broken by the far thunder of cannon in the west. The men of Rochester pulled their lanyards and the guns of the "Young Lion" spoke. Soon off to the east was heard the boom of the Pittsford salute.

Governor Clinton and his flotilla had left Buffalo on the triumphal tour that marked the formal opening of the Grand Canal.

The next day found Rochester in a ferment. Throngs converged on the canal banks near Exchange Street. Eight companies of militia in showy uniforms and under arms, turned out. So did a committee of leading citizens, headed appropriately enough by Jesse Hawley, who from a debtor's prison, had penned the first clarion call for a canal across the state.

At 2 p. m. four sleek grays trotted down the Towpath. They were hauling the flagship, Seneca Chief, on which De Witt Clinton was riding the glory road. In its wake were the Superior, the Perry and the Buffalo.

At Child's Basin, the Rochester packet, "Young Lion of the West" guarded the entrance. There ensued a ceremony patterned after the Masonic ritual. Was not Clinton the Grand Master of the order? From the Seneca Chief came the ceremonial challenge. From the Young Lion came the reply: "All right, pass." The Lion gave way, the Seneca Chief slid into the basin. Then pandemonium broke loose.

The militia fired their muskets. The cannon roared again. The crowds yelled. The Rochester and Canandaigua committees took their places under an arch surmounted by an eagle and the Seneca Chief was moored amid fervid oratory.

Then came dinner at the Mansion House in State Street, more speeches, many toasts and at 7:30 that night the visitors re-embarked. With the fleet sailed the "Young Lion of the West," with a distinguished Rochester committee aboard to take part in the historic 'wedding of the waters" nine days later at Sandy Hook.

* * * *

In 1825 Rochester had 4,274 inhabitants. Within a year the figure had jumped to 7,669. No other town in America was growing so rapidly. 'The Young Lion' was THE canal town, with 160 Rochester-owned boats and 882 Rochester-owned horses on the Ditch.

One day in 1826, 22 craft arrived here, among them: The New Hampshire, out of Brockport with ashes, flour and wheat; the General Putnam with merchandise from Albany, the Brandywine bearing wheat, ashes, whisky from Buffalo; the Sea Gull, out of Salina (Syracuse), with a cargo of salt, and the Echo, from Holley, carrying wheat. As many departed with varied cargoes. That year also, 100 live rattlesnakes were shipped from Rochester for the European market. Their oil was considered valuable.

* * * *

Then came the tumultuous 1830's when Rochester's population more than doubled, jumping from 9,000 to 20,000. During that decade the 27-year long, four million dollar enlargement of the canal was begun and work was started on the second Aqueduct. Clinton's Ditch had outgrown its baby clothes.

By 1835 Rochester owned or controlled half of the boats on the canal. Hundred of canal vessels were built in yards here.

It was in 1836 that a canal boat brought to Rochester a cargo of ominous import. It was the first locomotive for the Tonawanda

Railroad. The next year the first train rumbled out of the city for Attica. An interloper had arrived to challenge the supremacy of the waterway and to remain its relentless rival for many years.

* * * *

The second Aqueduct, a little to the south of the first, was begun in 1833 and completed in 1842 at a cost of about $444,000. This one did not leak. Most of it is there today, a part of the subway system. The structure, supported by seven arches, was 848 feet long and 45 feet wide to conform to the new dimensions of the Ditch. It was built of coniferous limestone, obtained at Split Rock near Syracuse.

* * * *

During the 1840's, the city's life swirled around Exchange Street and the canal. There the boats arrived and departed. There were the big hotels, the offices, warehouses and stores linked to the canal trade. To the south were lumber yards, soap and candle factories.

And there was the huge, rambling four-story Rochester House, catering to the packet trade. The packets brought some distinguished visitors, among them tourists, actors and statesmen. From the hotel's big balcony President Martin Van Buren and other notables of the time spoke.

It was a gaudy era and the packet boats gave it sparkle.

Edwin Scrantom, who was born in the first dwelling built on the 100-Acre Tract, on the site of the present Powers Building, gave the Historical Society when an old man this vivid picture of the arrival of a packet boat:

"A long, slim boat with its glass sides shining in the sun rounded and came into the Aqueduct, on the east side of the river. Her bow and stern, displaying ribbons and streamers, she dashes along, a thing of life, drawn by three over-driven horses, covered with a foam of sweat.

Rochester Aqueduct in "Good Old Days"

"Serene, Immaculate" Pittsford

"We can see, too, the lines of trunks along the docks on the outside and in the middle a standing congregation of gentlemen and ladies all agog, ready to see and be seen. We can hear, too, the nervous duet of two Kent bugles or maybe a band of music, heralding the incoming packet.

"The packet boat enters Child's Basin. Loafer Bridge is a mass of human beings. Handkerchiefs are displayed and answered from the boat. Cheers go up and the crowd, especially the boys, rush for the packet offices where cabmen, hackmen, porters and runners call for guests, scramble for hotels and make confusion worse confounded by their bickerings and blackguardisms."

In the 1840's a new span replaced the Loafer Bridge, so called because a character called Loafer Jim spent most of his time there, watching the boats. The new high bridge was difficult for horses and wagons to negotiate. The Rochester House burned down in 1853. It had lost much of its old elegance. Evangelists held services in its big parlor, preaching to the hard-boiled canallers. The railroads were driving the packets out of business.

A colorful era was dying and Exchange Street never was quite the same again.

*   *   *   *

In 1852 the weighlock was built, to be part of the canal scene for 70 years until it was torn down to make room for the subway. It was on the east side of the river on Crouch's Island, about opposite Capron Street. A two-story brick building, it had a stately portico with Doric pillars. Boats entered under this portico. Double gates at either end allowed the water to be drawn off and the tonnage taken by huge scales. Up to the time tolls were abolished in 1882, it was one of the busiest places along the Towpath.

*   *   *   *

The great flood of St. Patrick's Day, 1865, which took such heavy toll in the city, swept away the canal banks near the river.

Three years later the first steamer ever to traverse the waterway, the Edward Backus, built here and named after her owner, a Rochester man, brought a load of coal from Ithaca. It foreshadowed the eventual passing of the Towpath and four legged motive power, although that change was many years in coming.

Rivalry was so intense captains would hire crews for their fighting prowess rather than their seamanship. There were canal bullies all along the line. Ben Streeter was the Rochester bully. He lived at the Rapids, across the Genesee from the present River Campus and mostly worked on the old Genesee Valley Canal. Ben fought the bully of Buffalo in the Reynolds Arcade for one hour and licked him. The exact date of this classic battle is elusive.

But the late Capt. H. P. Marsh, canal veteran, in his delightful little book, "Rochester and Its Early Canal Days," recalled that "not an officer dared interfere."

The craft owned by the big companies were called line boats. They were likely to hire captains of the rougher sort. The captains engaged their own crews, men after their own hearts. Many of the independent owners who piloted their own boats were respectable and, some of them, pious men. They took their families along and their boats were neat and homelike.

But in general, the Erie Canal was no place for one who believed in the niceties.

Songs floated through the night from the Towpath, robust ballads, many of which are unprintable. The canallers creeping across the state, sang as marching soldiers do, "just to pass the time away."

Here is one of the better known ballads that has survived the changing years:

> "Lay me on the horse bridge,
>   With my feet turned to the bow;
> And let it be a Lockport laker
>   Or a Tonawanda scow.
> For the Erie, it is ragin'
>   And our gin is getting low;
> Oh, I hardly think we'll get a drink,
>   Till we get to Buffalo."

The last statement is sheer "poetic license" because there were grog shops at every lock.

There's another song titled "Boatin' on a Bull-Head." It must be explained that Bull-Head boats, many of which were built in Rochester yards, were built flush up to the cabin. The helmsman had to stand on the cabin roof to steer. There was little space between his post and the low bridges. So many a canaller was swept off to his death. The old ballad warns:

> "So canallers, take my warning:
>   Never steer a Bull-Head boat
> Or they'll find you some fair mornin'
>   In the Erie afloat.
> Do all your fine navigatin'
>   In the Line-barn full of hay,
> And the Low Bridge, you won't be hatin'
>   And you'll live to Judgment Day."

*   *   *   *

The later days of the canal were less picturesque. Politics and machinery and big combinations added materialistic touches. But when the Barge Canal was authorized in 1903 (incidentally against the violent opposition of Rochester interests) there were 4,000 boat owners on the waterway.

The burly figure of George W. Aldridge, longtime political boss of Rochester, strode the canal stage in the late 90's when he was state superintendent of public works. During his regime millions were appropriated for canal deepening and other improvements. The use of these funds was later investigated by Gov. Theodore Roosevelt who found "no cause for complaint." The horde of loyal Rochesterians who got canal jobs under Aldridge had no cause for complaint, either. Patronage fell like ripe fruit in a hail storm.

For 15 years the Barge Canal work went on. The new ditch, for 13 miles, from west of Pittsford to South Greece, skirted the city it once bisected. Some contractors made money. Some went broke. Digging the long "Rock Cut" west of the city was a heart-breaking job.

In 1912, agitation began in Rochester for abandonment of the canal bed within the city. But business interests along the route fought for its preservation. In 1919 the last boat passed through the Aqueduct. In 1920 the Ditch was declared formally abandoned.

Meanwhile, on May 10, 1918, State Engineer Williams had grabbed a shovel from a workman and opened a trench across a dike at the west bank of the river in Genesee Valley Park. Genesee water poured through to mingle with Erie water. The Barge Canal was proclaimed formally opened.

In 1921 the city authorized the electrified railroad in the old canal bed. The next year Mayor Van Zandt wielded a silver spade in the Ditch west of Oak Street. Rochester's $11,800,000 subway had been launched.

Just a century before the first flour-laden canal boat had left Hill's Basin.

*   *   *   *

I'll bet that subway conductor still is wondering about the bald-headed guy who rode the whole length of the subway—twice in one morning|

If his passenger had told him that "I'm not really riding the subway at all. I'm riding the Erie Canal and this is not 1945 but

30, 40, 50 years ago," the conductor surely would have called the wagon.

As the subway car sped along the tracks in the bed of the Clinton Ditch, I tried to recapture the yesterdays that hold fond memories for so many Rochesterians who are no longer young.

In fancy, boys were diving again off the crossover bridge, "the Hoggie'" at the Western Wildwaters; the "Old Calamity" lift bridge was up at West Avenue (West Main) and the chorus "that's why I'm late for work" came out of the past.

The little Jessie chugged along on the Fairport run, beer kegs piled high upon her deck; the C. H. Francis shuffled off for Buffalo with a mighty whistle blast that scared the farmer's horses crossing the Washington Street bridge.

Change the scene to winter and skaters were doing "the figure eight" on the Aqueduct skating rink and kids were playing "shinny" on the ice of the old canal feeder.

Canallers were buying soap and "suds" at the Adwen grocery at Lock 66 and lads were splashing merrily in the Eastern Widewaters and hitching rides from lock to lock.

A locktender and a mule driver were battling it out on the Towpath at Winton Road and the Caleys were shoeing canal mules in their blacksmith shop at the corners in old Brighton.

*   *   *   *

Want to go along on a dream trip in a memory-haunted ditch?

Let's start at the western terminal of the subway—and forget there is such a thing. The Western Widewaters, playground for generations of West Side youths, shimmer in the sunshine as of yore.

The younger kids splash around in the "baby hole" at the shallow end, but bolder souls dive from the "Hoggie Bridge," hard by Driving Park Avenue where the Towpath crosses from the north to the south side. Mischievous boys call out "Whoa, Johnny," and the mules all stop and the drivers swear eloquently.

At the western end of the waters is Scott's Bridge, carrying Field's Road over the canal. Max Straussner of Lisbon Street works today in the huge plant of the Rochester Products Division of General Motors on the southeastern edge of the former Widewaters. He recalls a day in 1900 when he dived off Scott's Bridge, then looked back a couple of minutes later to see the span collapse. It stayed down many a year until Mount Read Boulevard was completed, skirting the whole northwest side of the city. By then, the Widewaters had been filled in and were only memory.

At Lexington Avenue, the "Slanty Roof" tavern still stands but it serves the factory trade and not thirsty canallers. Once it was Hartleben's and later Johnson's. Arthur W. Johnson of the Fire Bureau, son of Otto Johnson, once proprietor of the tavern, called up boyhood recollections of rented rowboats and small launches, manned by anglers, swarming the Widewaters on summer Sundays.

The hobo jungle in the woods to the west; the canal boats tied up for the winter and families living on them; the cinder path beloved of bicyclists; sunken barges from which kids, playing hookey from classes, dived—they are all part of the Widewaters tradition.

And the skating in winter time and the Hetzlers cutting ice. The Hetzler plant still is there and Leo Hetzler is head of the company his father established beside the Widewaters 78 years ago.

Trek north by west to Ridgeway Avenue and you see again the Four Mile Grocery, called by canal men "the hard cider stop." Years ago it vanished from the scene but the old canal banks all along the "Big Ridge" are still visible.

The canal, riding the "Big Ridge," was on higher ground than the land to the north and old timers who lived in the lower regions recall how strange it was to see moving canal boats silhouetted against the sky as they looked upward.

* * * *

"Nothing provokes so much profanity in Rochester as the canal bridges. Captains apparently wait until morning, noon and evening rushes are on to start through the waterway with their boats. Cars are blocked for street after street and pedestrians and bicyclists are equally inconvenienced."

So fumed an editorial in the Rochester Herald in 1903.

Possibly the writer had "Old Calamity" at the present intersection of West Main, Broad and Clarissa in mind.

In the 1870's there was an overhead bridge which also spanned the old Genesee Valley Canal, 300 feet away. The heavy grades necessitated the use of a hill horse for the horse street cars. Then a swing bridge came, to be supplanted by a lift bridge in 1889. The last "Old Calamity" lasted as long as the old canal did. It should have been dubbed "Old Alibi" because for years it formed a rock-ribbed excuse for being late at the office or shop.

Once it got stuck while down and would not go up for days, piling up traffic on the waterway for miles in either direction. Once "Calamity" tossed one of its weigh boxes, filled with chunks of iron, on the roof of a trolley. It was only a glancing blow and none of the passengers was hurt save those trampled in the rush for exits.

There were a lot of those lift bridges in Rochester and they had considerable to do with the abandonment of the Ditch through the downtown section.

The Washington Street bridge was an overhead span with steep approaches that tested the power of automobiles in the infancy of the horseless carriage. A Virginia creeper twined around it.

From the old bridge the elegant ladies of the Third Ward watched for the packet boats bringing home their men from sessions of the Legislature at Albany or financial deals in New York. The old Ditch was the northern boundary of the "Ruffled Shirt" domain.

In later days, Mechanics Institute art students used to sketch around the bridge. From the Washington Street dock and warehouse, the stone building that now houses a restaurant and a religious sect, the steam freight packets used to depart for east and west.

* * * *

The time has come to talk of many things, including ships that carried shoes and sealing wax and cabbages but nary a king.

The steam freight packets ran through the 1890's up until around 1905 when the new Barge Canal had doomed the Towpath.

Maybe the names of some of the boats will evoke memories —the William B. Kirk, the C. H. Francis, the John Owens, the Charles J. Johnson, the Milton S. Price, condemned and supplanted by the Celena, the fruit boat; the O. B. Tanner, the Graham, the J. M. Wiltsie, the Whipple, the little Jessie, the Frankie Reynolds and the Rambler among them.

For their animal-powered contemporaries, the steam packet men had a contemptuous word, "Hayburners."

The packets carried all manner of merchandise and stopped at every canal town where merchants relied on them for most of their supplies. In fall they bore away tons of produce and fruit. Storing that freight according to destination was an art. There also was a vast amount of clerical work involved in checking and making out way bills, usually the task of the captain-purser.

Harry A. Wood, 71, who lives in Roslyn Street, for ten years served the Buffalo and Rochester Transit Company in that capacity and how his eyes kindled as he looked over old pictures of the boats. He told how the girls in the Kimball factory, now City Hall Annex, would toss out tobacco to passing boatmen; how his boss, Judson Webster, co-owner of the line with Henry Chamberlin of Buffalo, rode the Towpath on his bicycle checking his boats; how the bank watchers would report pilots exceeding the speed limit, for too much speed caused swells that might wash away canal banks.

There were occasional passengers. Sometimes they paid. Sometimes they rode free. The captains did not care much. Freight was their business.

And for years the canal boats waged war with the powerful railroads that paralleled the Ditch. It was an unequal struggle. For the rail lines would lower their rates during the canal season and raise them at its close. There was no Interstate Commerce Commission or tariff regulatory body in those days.

The Webster-Chamberlin interests sold out around 1899 and some of their boats and others were operated by the Buffalo, Rochester and Syracuse line, headed by George Hall. This line gave up the ghost in 1905.

I spent some time chasing around the countryside looking up canal men, never knowing there were two canallers right in my office. One of them is Fred Masterson, the night cashier, who was captain of the C. H. Francis in 1903, and the other, his nephew, Howard Kemp, the fish and game columnist, who that year, although a mere boy, worked as a deckhand.

The Francis had a capacity of 100 tons and plied between Buffalo and Syracuse. Captain Fred recalls one time that busy fall of '03 when the crew, tired out from juggling freight at every port, found waiting them at lower Lockport 525 cases of canned goods and at upper Lockport a huge heap of iron castings and a barrel of pitch.

Sometimes the boats carried excursionists, usually to groves near Spencerport and Fairport in the days of peek-a-boo waists, picture hats and buttoned shoes.

Once the William B. Kirk, celebrated as an excursion craft, broke away from its moorings at the feeder and was swept down the river. It wound up with its bow way out over the Court Street dam. The weight of the machinery in the stern kept it from going all the way.

In the autumns of some 35 years ago University of Rochester students used to charter canal boats to take them to the Varsity-Hamilton football games at Clinton, near Utica. In 1910, among the passengers on such a trip on the good ship Rambler, were three men now connected with the Rochester school system, James M. Spinning, superintendent of schools; John M. Merrell of East High and J. Jenner Hennessy of Franklin High. Others were Frank Wells, the insurance man; Axel Gay of Eastman Kodak and Ellis Gay of East Rochester.

The Rambler stopped in Syracuse. The students had dinner and went to a show but the crew evidently found other forms of entertainment. Let Hennessy tell the tale of the night ride to Utica:

"The Erie itself was quiet and serene but what it failed to furnish in excitement was supplied by the antics of the boat. The west-bound traffic was heavy that night. There wasn't a west bound craft that we did not meet either broadside or head on. Along toward morning the Rambler tried to hurdle the line between a tug and a tow. Then when the westbound boats got scarce, we just rammed one bank or the other."

But the collegians reached Utica in time to see Rochester wallop Hamilton 5 to 2.

In the fall of 1919, the Towpath Era ended when Capt. Marion S. Kelsey piloted the William B. Kirk through the Aqueduct. On Dec. 2, 1927 Canaller Kelsey rode the first car to flash through the city's new $12,000,000 subway.

* * * *

Through the downtown section, busy Broad Street hides the

old canal bed from view. Remember the battle over the name of the new street over the subway some 18 years ago and the determined group that fought to the last for "Towpath?"

We are underground at Exchange Street, once the core of canal activities. But in fancy we can see old Capt. Dick Patterson and his "one-man life saving station" there. Dick for years was a flagman at the lift bridge. Somehow the Towpath was never wide enough for some tavern habitues and nobody knows how many of them Dick fished out of the canal. On his shanty hung a life preserver and on his coat many medals for his rescues.

* * * *

The old Aqueduct was a gay place in the winters of the 1890's and the early days of the new century. As soon as canal navigation ended, it was made ready for outdoor skating. The rink was formed by placing sand bags at either end of the Aqueduct to retain about two feet of water in the channel. A shed was put up and a stove installed. On the stove a pail of hot water was kept at boiling point, so that skates might be dipped and cleaned of ice and snow to prevent rust.

Rocker skates with steel runners fastened to wooden tops were in vogue. Some had elaborate designs in curled steel at the toes. A few "tony" kids had skates permanently attached to boots but strap skates were the rule. There were gala nights when a band played and 10 cents admission was charged. The last trolley left at midnight and there was a hasty exodus from the rink just before the stroke of .12.

As the subway car rushed through the 100-year-old arched structure at the noon hour, in fancy I heard merry voices and saw whirling figures of other noon hours long ago. Business and professional men would gulp down sandwiches and coffee to spend the rest of their free time on the rink, to join the boys and girls in doing "the outer edge" and other fancy numbers.

* * * *

The old canal feeder that ran from South Avenue to the railroad underpass north of the present River Campus also is enshrined in many memories. There many an East Side lad, among them Columnist Henry W. Clune, played "shinny" in winter, fished for bullheads and swam in long-gone summers. There they fought invading gangs from Swillburg and from the Rapids. What is now River Boulevard was a rough dirt road beside the feeder. But there was a good bicycling path and Heinie Clune remembers seeing Bert Lytell, a matinee idol of the time, fishing in the old feeder after riding a bike up from his hotel.

* * * *

The Ditch was the northern boundary of the area known in other days as Swillburg, the Meigs-Clinton sector. The early German settlers there, and fine, thrifty citizens they were, kept pigs, hence the name. The canal served them well. They would get water out of the Ditch with rope and bucket. They used the silt from its bed for their gardens in the spring and got crabs and other bait for fishing there.

Mrs. L. D. Potter of Thurston Court is one of thousands of Rochesterians to whom mention of the Erie Canal brings acute nostalgia. She spent her girlhood in a house on Broadway, a few doors from the one her grandfather, William Smith, built when he came here from Schenectady by packet boat in 1831. He and his sons after him had a boat yard near by.

She treasures girlhood memories of parents telling little girls to shun the Towpath and its rough mule drivers, and warning little boys never to swim in the canal that had claimed so many young lives; music of the German band floating across the Ditch from Swillburg on a Sunday afternoon; children waving at the Jessie from the Averill Avenue bridge and the Norwegian ship, the Viking, bound for the World's Fair at St. Louis, halted at the bridge for a little time and the whole neighborhood out to see it.

Hollyhocks nod their bright heads from the Towpath and the Heelpath, too, as the subway cars roar past old Lock 66 and one sees the stones of the old lock mingling with the concrete of the subway wall.

There stands one of the last tangible links with the old Ditch —the Adwen canal grocery. One of the last along the whole waterway to close, it ended its canal career in 1917. The first Stephen Adwen built it there a century ago—the long, low, weather-beaten building with the old fashioned blinds, now facing the high speed subway railroad as it faced the lazy Erie water for so many years.

The old building only recently passed out of the hands of the Adwen family. The third Stephen Adwen and his brother, George, were born in the place and have vivid recollections of the canallers who stopped for groceries, soap and beverages.

It's hard to find the landmark unless you walk what once was the Towpath. It's at the end of Adwen Place. Adwen Place is an extension of Rutgers Street and it is not a city throughfare. The first Adwen once owned the land all the way to Monroe Avenue. When Rutgers Street was built, the Adwens reserved 500 feet at the southern end. Today it is an unpaved private street with only three houses on it beside the historic grocery.

At the old lock site is the footbridge high over the subway that was built, through the efforts of Father Thomas F. Connors after the canal was abandoned, for the benefit of the children of Blessed Sacrament School who lived south of the erstwhile waterway.

*   *   *   *

And now we come to the Eastern Widewaters—"The Wides" they used to call them when Dr. Clint W. La Salle was an East Side boy in the 1880s.

A small part of the old "Wides" is preserved in the sparkling little lake variously called Lake Riley, Cobb's Hill Lake and Eastern Widewaters. I believe the last is still the official name.

The Eastern Widewaters never had the large following of their western neighbor but they had an intensely loyal one. The West Side was built up earlier than the far East Side and Culver Road was a long way out when grandpa was a boy and the trolleys only ran to Alexander Street.

But the Eastern "Wides" outlived the rival western playground and for decades has been a mecca for skaters, swimmers and lovers of peaceful beauty.

The waters once extended as far as Colby Street, where Sam Hart had a saw mill and covered the present Armory site on which once were a motor engine factory and a boat works.

And in the days when Canterbury Road was Pacific Street, the Kondolf ice houses were there and the Kondolf ice pond covered what is now Harvard Street and adjacent area.

At the Eastern Widewaters, once the turning basin for the canal boats, stands a cairn made from stones of the first Aqueduct and placed there on the 100th anniversary of the completion of Clinton's Ditch.

*   *   *   *

"Eight minutes to City Hall" reads a sign on the subway station in Winton Road in Old Brighton.

Go up to the old cemetery on the hill where sleep the pioneers of Brighton Village and stand under the old trees of the pleasant street that leads to it and you are removed years in time and miles in space from City Hall and the clangor of the city.

You will see there the tomb of William C. Bloss, who in early days ran the three-story red brick tavern that stood beside the canal until the subway came and was known as Miller's and then as Sheehan's. Bloss sickened of the business and, as is recorded on the stone, dumped all the liquor from his tavern into the canal. He became a foremost temperance advocate as well as a champion of the anti-slavery and woman suffrage causes. He died in 1863.

Up there on the hill is the stately yellow brick colonial home that pioneer William Perrin built around 1828, the second oldest house in Brighton village. The oldest is the stone dwelling at 1885 East Ave. with its back to the canal that Brightonians call the "Plaster House." Perrin built that too—in the first lush days of the canal boom.

Back in 1842, Thomas Caley opened a blacksmith and wagon shop at East Avenue and Winton Road. They called it "Caley's Corner." For 103 years the Caleys have been there, three generations of them, switching to automobiles when the horse and buggy days passed. Three grandsons of Thomas Caley hold forth at the old stand, Frank, Morrill and William.

Morrill chanced to be the one I approached in my quest of Brighton lore. He was born virtually on the bank of the canal. Morrill Caley remembers as a boy hearing the drivers singing on the Towpath. Some of them had good voices and some of them even sang hymns. He told of the high bridge that once spanned the canal at Winton Road and how boys used to slide down it on their sleds, right across East Avenue and the Central tracks; of the winter rink between the two eastern locks and the ice harvest there.

Brighton was a roaring canal town in its day with three locks and several hotels and saloons. One lock was at the present Colby Street, another called Sipple's after the grocery there, at Winton and a third, just to the east and known as Miller's. Bussey's was the hotel that is now O'Hara's; the East Avenue once was Case's and the Brighton, with its back to the old Ditch, was Madigan's. All of them knew the Erie "when it was a'raging."

But that was when Brighton, the three-lock port, was by no means, "eight minutes from City Hall."

"Rowlands. End of the line," sang out the subway man in blue.

There the subway ends but the old Ditch goes on, to join the new Barge west of Pittsford.

It is 1945 again. The dream trip is ended.

But the memories linger on.

Mother of Monroe

PITTSFORD, tidy, tranquil "white village" at Rochester's eastern portal, is a different sort of canal town.

Pittsford is no child of the Erie Canal. She was born in the 18th Century in the wake of the Revolution, when the Ditch was but a dream. She was a thriving settlement when Rochester was a miasmic mudhole.

She is the mother town of all Monroe County. She had the first school, the first library, the first lawyer, the first physician in what is now the County of Monroe.

A casual visitor today might dismiss Pittsford as just part of the city. Once all the present city east of the Genesee River was a part of Pittsford, when the village was the center of the mother township variously known as Northfield, Boyle and Smallwood.

To be sure, the digging of the Ditch made the village an important produce shipping port and spurred her growth. Yet Pittsford, of her own choosing, has remained a smallish residential village. Today she has no industries save a pickle factory and a flour mill. She wants no clouds of factory smoke, no babel of foreign tongues. Her population of 1,544 (1940 census) is a blend of city folk, many of them people of means, and of natives, many of them descendants of the New England settlers.

Only eight miles to the west roars an industrial city of a third of a million. Yet "The Mother of Monroe" has remained unsullied, immaculate and herself.

I like to think of Pittsford as "The White Village." She is like a white lily, lifting her stately head proudly amid newer, bigger, showier blooms in the garden of villages.

Ghosts walk "The White Village."

Over the old Seneca trail, Denonville's French and Indian legions march again as they did that July day of 1687, to encamp at the Big Spring on their way to battle the Keepers of the Western Door.

We see, too, the tribesmen stopping by the spring on their way from Irondequoit Bay to their villages in the hinterland in the days when all this domain was theirs.

The year is 1789 and the Stone cousins, Simon and Israel, Revolutionary veterans, build the first white man's habitation near that same Big Spring in State Street.

To later generations the site was known as Plumb's Pond and church baptismal rites were conducted there. Then the Barge Canal came and spring and pond went into its maw.

But when the canal is drained in the off-season, the Big Spring can still be seen bubbling out of its depths.

In 1790 other Revolutionary veterans followed the Stones, among them Capt. Henry Gale, sentenced to hang for his part in Shay's Massachusetts Rebellion and later pardoned. He was the great-great-grandfather of Zona Gale, the novelist, and in her lifetime the Wisconsin writer saw to it that the captain's grave in Pittsford cemetery was well tended.

The first physician, Dr. John Ray, arrives in 1792 and we see him riding the rough trails on horseback. Two years later the first schoolhouse is built south of the village. Some of the settlers own slaves and Negro youngsters sit with the white children in the little classroom.

In 1803 a library is established in the old house that still stands at the foot of Tobey Hill. The next year Simon Stone, the first lawyer, hangs out his shingle.

Then, in 1807, a pretentious three-story hotel with wide porches and a spring ballroom on its top floor rises at the Four Corners. It is called the Phoenix and stage coaches roll up to its doors. It's still there after 138 years; the ballroom is gone, so are the porches and it's known now as the Pittsford Inn.

What famous ghosts haunt that old tavern. There's De Witt Clinton, stopping there while exploring the route for his Ditch; then after the canal is done, there's Lafayette on his tour of 1825. The aging hero of the Revolution leaves the waterway at Rochester and is taken by carriage to Canandaigua. Rochester has no equipage fine enough, so it is the carriage of James K. Guernsey of Pittsford that bears the famous visitor southward. A few years later the silver-tongued Daniel Webster rides in the same coach and stays at the same inn. A night in 1826 sees another carriage pull up, men push a huddled figure into the dining room, eat hastily and depart. The mysterious guest is William Morgan, the Anti-Mason, abducted from Canandaigua Jail and soon to disappear at Fort Niagara.

A young pedestrian, Edward Payson Weston, stays at the inn in 1867, without fanfare. Fifty years later the same man, a world famous hiker at 84, returns, to the cheers of a crowd.

Gay dances in the old ball room, political rallies, florid oratory, fugitive slaves hidden in the cellar—few buildings hereabouts have the glamorous history of Pittsford's 138-year old inn.

When I visited Pittsford, workmen were completing the razing of the three-story building that once was known as the White Tavern and was built in 1818, beside the first Clinton Ditch.

The stately red brick house with the broad lawns at 52 South Main Street, now the home of Mr. and Mrs. Theodore C. Briggs, was erected in 1812. Augustus Elliott, the distiller, built it for his bride-to-be, a daughter of the house of Penfield. She jilted him and Elliott never lived in the mansion. It has had several owners but it is best known as the Hargous house. When the family of that name lived there in pre-Civil War days, the spacious cellar hid many a fugitive Negro, bound for Canada and freedom.

In this village there are many mansions, few of them gaudy. There are many tasteful white Colonial homes and there are white picket fences in the New England manner.

Is not this village named after a town in old Vermont whence came many of her settlers?

* * * *

The first Ditch followed the line of the present South Street. Several houses on that thoroughfare stand squarely over the old bed. The enlarged Erie and the Barge Canal were built some distance to the east.

At the southeast corner of South and State Streets is a brick dwelling that was a canal grocery. The cellar door that was once at the level of the first Ditch is now bricked up.

Frank W. Pugsley, lean, kindly mayor of Pittsford, is also town and village historian. This former metallurgical engineer for the Hiram Sibley western mining interests, and before that a hand on his uncle's ranch in the Indian Territory, is a native son, a veritable mine of lore of the village and of the canal.

He is an "old canaller" himself. In his youth he briefly tended old Lock 62 which was just west of the village and one summer he was a flagman on the Exchange Street bridge in Rochester. His father, James Pugsley, tended a lock on the old Erie east of Pittsford.

From his father Frank Pugsley heard many a strange story of Erie water. The most fantastic is the tale of the fighting lice. Two canal men met in a Pittsford grog shop. Each had a pet louse which he had trained to fight. Each slapped his warrior down on the bar. The drinks were on the loser. A crowd watched the battle. Finally one tiny fighter emerged the victor. The proud owner fondly restored the champion to his person, ready for the next fray.

There were other canallers who on moonlight nights would tie up near a farmer's field, dig row after row of potatoes and flee with their booty. Others who, when farmers' ducks swam near their boats, would bait a line with corn and haul in the birds.

The mayor told of an entirely different sort of canal character, a boat captain who would never run on Sundays, who attended church every Sabbath with his wife wherever his craft was tied up; who would tolerate neither profanity nor drinking in his crew.

Pugsley spoke of the painting done by the British artist, George Harvey, in 1837 which hangs in the State Historical Society's Museum in Cooperstown. It depicts a packet boat, drawn by trotting horses, rounding King's Bend, near Sutherland's woods, west of Pittsford. Historian Pugsley identified the scene for the state society when a New York art dealer listed the painting for sale.

*   *   *   *

There's an oldtime canaller living in Pittsford, in the white house on Monroe Avenue next to the Village Building. His name is Tom Heaver.

For nearly a decade, during the closing days of the Erie, he was a captain and licensed pilot on the steam freight packets. There are few of those pilots left. Heaver served on the J. M. Wiltsie, owned

In Wake of Bushnell Basin "Break"

Fairport, a "Cradle of Industry"

and launched in Pittsford; on the C. H. Francis, the Lewis M. Lawrence and the O. B. Tanner. They plied mostly between Buffalo and Syracuse.

The broad-shouldered, good humored captain has many memories of the old canal days; of the time the Wiltsie nearly broke in two at its launching through a workman's mistake as it slid down the ways; of the grain boat built in Pittsford that swelled and burst years ago; of seeing dead mules and horses floating in the Ditch, tossed there when their shoulder galls were too severe to pass the inspection of the canal veterinaries; of crafty owners who put blankets on their animals to hide the sores, claiming the covering was to keep off flies; of fights on the Towpath, mostly caused by green horses or mules crowding.

Tom Heaver cherishes recollections of the last banquet of the Society of the Erie Canal, in Albion in 1939. Some 200 people were there but Tom and the late Dr. Frank Lattin of Gaines were the only bona fide canallers in the crowd.

The Society of the Erie Canal was conceived in a spirit of fun as a purely social organization. It was a "take off" on the august and dignified Society of the Genesee which before the war used to hold elaborate annual banquets in New York, with a dazzling array of white starched shirt front.

Membership in the Society of the Erie Canal is limited to those who worked on the waterway or lived on its banks or swam, fished or skated on its waters.

Let's hope that with the advent of peace the society will be revived. I propose Capt. Tom Heaver of Pittsford for honorary chief engineer.

By the way, I wonder if, by virtue of my tugboat ride, I am not eligible to membership?

*   *   *   *

There's a Pittsford tale in which Heaver figures and which has naught to do with the Erie Canal.

Some 50 years ago when Tom and Dr. Irving Crump, the dentist, were young men, they were hired to dig a well in Locust Street near South. After getting through the Pittsford shale, a geological formation peculiar to the locality, they encountered thick rock which they blasted. Some 50 feet down they uncovered a natural cavern. A man could walk through it. The well diggers explored it with a lantern as far as the Four Corners, where it branched off. Then they quit. Nobody knows its extent. So this intriguing village has a secret labyrinth, too.

A notable native son was the late Admiral William F. Fullam, born in Pittsford in 1855. He served in the Spanish-American War and first World War. In the war of 1918 he was a member of the potent Navy Board and a pioneer exponent of the use of air power in naval warfare. He died in Washington in 1926.

In the 1830s, young Dr. Hartwell Carver began the practice of medicine in the village. He was no ordinary country doctor. He was a man with a dream—that of a transcontinental railroad. He bombarded Congress and men of influence with letters and personal pleas for thirty years. Finally in 1869 he saw his dream come true when the Union Pacific was completed. An imposing monument stands in Mount Hope Cemetery in Rochester, erected by the grateful state of California to the "Father of the Pacific Railroad."

*   *   *   *

In the sunshine of a perfect August afternoon—on a day when the Rising Sun of pagan empire was setting in the Pacific—Mayor Pugsley and I walked from Pittsford to Bushnell's Basin and return. We went by way of what once was the Heelpath and took the Towpath trail back.

We detoured a bit to visit the ghost port of Cartersville, a mile and a quarter from Pittsford. The Barge Canal bypassed Cartersville and only some farm buildings remain where once was an important canal and railroad shipping port. Gone are the warehouse, the docks, the basin, the big distillery with its tramway over the highway to the tracks of the Auburn Road. Gone are the pens beside the distillery where bulls were fed the surplus mash, fattened and sold.

Frank Pugsley recalled a night in 1878 when he was a young lad and from his home on Pugsley Hill, south of Pittsford, saw smoke billowing up from Cartersville. His father saddled a horse and was off for the fire. He came back with a tale of volunteer firemen rolling out 200 of the 250 barrels of prime Genesee Valley whisky in the distillery, emptying some of them on the spot until many a firefighter collapsed and not from smoke. Whisky was taken away in every kind of container. Meanwhile, the distillery burned to the ground.

J. Sheldon Fisher of Fisher's, an inveterate collector of regional lore, who now lives in Pittsford, told me that the first locomotive for the Auburn and Rochester Railroad came to Cartersville by canal boat in 1842.

* * * *

East of Pittsford and north of the canal is the succession of low, humpy hills known to geologists as the Pittsford esker. The range, nearly a half mile long, is rich in deposits of pure gravel and has yielded many tons.

* * * *

West of Bushnell's Basin for about a mile stands what was called in the olden times "The Great Embankment". It is a magnificent monument to the men who built the canal.

Doubting Thomases said the canal could never be carried across the Irondequoit Valley. But in this first survey in 1808 James

Geddes found the natural route and the canal, in tts various evolutions, has never departed from it.

Gaze up at the great bank, 70 feet high, from the highway paralleling the canal on the north side, consider it was built by wheelbarrows, picks and shovels and you take off your hat to the men who made the Clinton Ditch.

In 1818 the stupendous four-year task was begun. The dirt for the great fill was taken from the nearby hills and fields—in wheelbarrows. Each barrow crew was led by a "pacer" and every man had to keep up with him. Residents of the neighborhood turned out to help the Irish and the other diggers and some of the region's wealthiest farmers in later years were heard to boast that they once worked on the Erie Canal for 75 cents a day.

Pugsley told how one Yankee contractor took the job at 10 cents a yard; sublet the contract for five cents and pocketed a small fortune without turning a hand.

At first the trough of the embankment was floored with heavy square timbers resting on piles driven into the soft earth. Historians differ on how long that lumber lasted. Later the aqueduct was lined with stone and when the Barge Canal was built, the trough was made of solid concrete, at tremendous cost.

The great fill has seen many breaks. The soil in the bank is sandy; sometimes muskrats made the holes that sent the Erie waters rushing over the farmlands.

The most costly break came on the morning of Sept. 3, 1912 while the transition to the Barge Canal was under way. It was the scene of a similar washout a year before.

The old culvert which carried Irondequoit Creek under the canal suddenly gave way. A score of workmen had a close call. One was caught in the avalanche of earth and water but was lugged to safety by his comrades. Thousands of tons of water poured out on the farm lands, between the new steel guard gate at Cartersville and the old one at Bushnell's Basin.

Damage to machinery was heavy. Huge slabs of concrete were strewn along the line of the break. The washout came at the height of grain shipping on the waterway. State officials rushed to the scene. The break was repaired in five weeks. It cost the state some $250,000.

Now at either side of the canal at the scene of that washout of 1912 is a manhole that leads down about 50 feet to a tunnel along the bank where the canal employes may check the Great Embankment for breaks.

* * * *

The Irondequoit Valley is picturesque as seen from the canal bank. The creek sings demurely at the base of the great fill; once it hummed with saw and grist mills. Only the mill house of Jaeschke, the last miller, remains along the route. The mill was razed when the Barge was built.

At the end of the Great Embankment, in the pleasant valley, lies Bushnell's Basin, once a teeming port, now a quiet hamlet.

It has a bit of summer colony air. City people have built modern cottages amid the century-old buildings. Youngsters in bathing suits were playing along the canal.

Turn back the clock a century and you see farmers' wagons lined up for half a mile waiting to unload their potatoes, grain and other produce at the docks. Bushnell's Basin, named after a pioneer merchant, was one of the busiest shipping points in the area. Wagons, laden with gunpowder, rumbled down from the Powder Mills, now a county park. They took back willow lumber shipped in for the mills, for willow charcoal was a necessary ingredient for making blasting powder.

Two landmarks remain to tell of the Basin's heydey. One is a cobblestone warehouse, now a part of a vinegar works. It goes back to the first Ditch which once swashed against its back. The Barge takes a more northerly course.

The other landmark is the yellow and white, 2½-story tavern building with the pillared porches across its front and the tall chimneys. Built in the first days of the Clinton Ditch, it was a famous canal hotel with a spring dance floor that swayed to tripping feet. Once it is said, the swell caused by a fast moving canal boat would send the Erie water surging into its taproom. Solomon Brodt kept the hotel in early days and in later years John Cossow. William Cogswell, founder of a prominent Rochester family, was born there in 1824.

A dozen years ago a nudist group rented the historic place and held forth there. But not for long. An aroused neighborhood, bred in the New England tradition, drove the nudists out. Now the old hotel, a charming relic of the past, is a private residence.

* * * *

It had been a memorable hike, the six miles from Pittsford to Bushnell's Basin, and return.

Pugsley was as fresh as a daisy. The tired member of the pedestrian duo at journey's end was not the sinewy mayor of Pittsford.

It was yours truly, twenty years his junior.

The Fair Port

ONE hundred and twenty years ago, the pioneers, for perfectly obvious reasons, named their canal-spawned village Fairport.

It is a fair port in a green land, this industrial-residential town that is 10 miles from Rochester by highway and 17 by canal.

It is a sort of milepost in our Towpath ramble. For one thing, it is the first village on the Main Line—pierced by the steel ribbons of the main line of the imperial New York Central, ancient rival of the Ditch.

At Fairport the contour of the land changes. The Towpath lies now in the shadow of picturesque hills, on the threshold of the mystical land of the drumlins. To me, a congenital hillbilly, the quiet ruggedness of the hills was a welcome relief after so many miles of flat country.

In this canal town, industrial history has been written through the years. Fairport might well be called an industrial laboratory. No atoms have been smashed, but a remarkable variety of products, some of them revolutionary in their time, have originated and been manufactured there. Packages bearing the label, "Made in Fairport, N. Y." have found their way to far places.

Men of Fairport, skilled with their hands, venturesome, dogged, practical dreamers, wrought in little shops. They experimented through "long days of labor and nights devoid of ease." They invented and manufactured things and shipped them, in the beginning on the canal. Sometimes the little shops became huge plants and princely fortunes were made. Sometimes they yielded to changing times and vanished.

Some of the products that in other years made Fairport famous are no longer made there but the Main Line-canal town is still an important manufacturing center. And her industries still sprawl besides the tideless Erie water that made the town.

* * * *

This industrial village is also a community of neat homes and thrifty home owners. Fairport is a substantial sort of town, proud of its self-supporting municipal water and electric light systems. It has a sound civic spirit.

Many Rochesterians, among them junior and industrial executives, have recently bought homes in the village and are taking an active interest in its affairs. Others, renters, merely work in Rochester and sleep in Fairport. The community has a considerable Italian-American population. There also are many descendants of early settlers in the town.

* * * *

Shunning the marshy lowlands where now the village stands, the first settlers of the Town of Perinton took to the southern foothills.

The earliest, Glover Perrin, after whom the township was named, settled in 1789 on the Wapping (Ayrault) Road. More pioneers, mainly of the New England stock, braved the rigors of the frontier and a little community called Egypt was born in the hills.

In a lean year the settlers there had the only corn in the region and supplied other pioneers from near and far. So, knowing their Bible, they called the place Egypt.

Palmyra, "Drenched in History"

Fox Sisters and Birthplace of Spiritualism; The Mormon Shrine on "The Sacred Hill"

In the loftiest hills, in the early days, there lived a band of squatters, so lawless and wild that they were called the Turks. Finally their more substantial neighbors ended this squatter sovereignty and the Turks departed. But there's still a Turk Hill in the Perinton range. Baker Hill, said to be the highest in the county, towers above it. Thirty years ago Bausch & Lomb of Rochester had an observatory there. Keck's Hill is the familiar scene of motorcycle hill climbs.

The peaceful grandeur of the Perinton Hills has been extolled by Thomas Thackeray Swinburne, the poet of the Genesee, in this verse:

"From out the stillness, far away,
The church bells faintly ring,
But sweeter is the Sabbath day
Where chorus of wild birds sing.
Away! To rove and rest upon
The purple hills of Perinton."

*   *   *   *

But we must away from the purple hills and back to the lowlands and the Clinton Ditch and the 1820's.

Before the canal came, what is now a village of some 4,700 souls was a scattering of seven log houses, a frame house and a block-house. In 1822 the packet Myron Holley threaded its way through the narrow Ditch and tied up at Bushnell's Basin. And Fairport was born.

It was the familiar story. The growth of Egypt in the hills was abruptly arrested and stores, houses, mills, warehouses, docks sprang up around the four canal bridges in the lowlands.

To the west of Fairport was Fullam's Basin, later called Fullamtown. It challenged the supremacy of Fairport for a decade and had the first postoffice. But soon the settlement around the present Main Street bridge absorbed Fullam's, as it did the eastern rival, Peters' Bridge or Landing, later known as Cobb's. Farther to the east was Lyndon's (Knapp's) Bridge, once a busy place.

A footpath between the cabins of the Sperbeck brothers, John, on the site of the present Town Hall, and Martin, on the South Main Street hill, became the village's Main Street. Fairport men began building boats and operating them. As if touched by a magic wand, a bustling settlement blossomed beside the waterway.

In 1827 the whole community turned out for a three-day celeration incident to the raising of the Prichard Tavern. Walter Edmonds in his novel, Chad Hanna, has his hero spending part of his honeymoon at this inn. Later it was renamed the Fairport Hotel. The building, no longer a hostelry and remodeled into the Millstone Block, still stands on Main Street, a link with pioneer days.

* * * *

Perinton has an active historical society which has unearthed much lore of the town. Among its leaders are Mrs. Marjorie Snow Merriman, who lives opposite the historic site of Perrin's first cabin; Albert B. Hupp, civic-minded, retired business man; Miss Adelaide Clark and Town Clerk Charlotte Clapp. Thanks to the society's researches, we catch these echoes of the olden time:

The east-bound canal boats sounding their horns at Fullam's Basin, the number of blasts denoting the number of fresh horses needed at the boat barns of Fairport—the first Hannan, James, settling in 1810 at what is still Hannan's Corners—The days when Perinton was the leading potato growing town in America—The district school on the Palmyra Road that one winter when the boats were "frozen in" was attended by canallers, who were so unruly a husky male teacher was hired—the Curtis Pond on the Macedon Center Road where baptismal services were held and the Sunday in 1850 when the wooden railing around the pond gave way, sending many into the water for an involuntary baptism—the entry in the 1835 account book of Tomlinson & Peters, early canal shippers, to wit: "For services while painting boat at Rochester, 6 days, $6; board while painting boat, 6 days, $3."

* * * *

The Historical Society collection of old documents includes a pamphlet dated 1828 and captioned in bold letters, "Remember the Sabbath Day, to keep it holy." Signed by some 30 influential Western New Yorkers and adopted at a Rochester meeting of "Friends of the Fourth Commandment," the manifesto resolves that "we are of one heart and one mind on this subject and will use our best exertions to prevent the violation of the Lord's Day on the Erie Canal" and pledges that "we will give our business and patronage to such lines of boats as do not travel on the Lord's Day."

But still the horn of the boatmen continued to challenge the peal of the church bells on the Sabbath mornings of 1828.

* * * *

Fairport's first industry, other than the inevitable saw and grist mills, was an unusual and short lived one. It was a mulberry grove at Main and Church streets for raising silk worms, with an adjacent silk factory.

In 1852 a former canal boat captain, Daniel B .De Land, established a saleratus plant on the banks of the canal. The next year the railroad that later became the New York Central was built. Both events were significant.

For many years the De Land plant was the village's principal industry and the De Lands the influential family. Cap-Sheaf soda was shipped all over the world and in the heyday of the industry, 200 men were employed by De Land's.

The business had a humble beginning. At first D. B. De Land drove a horse and wagon from house to house collecting the wood ashes that were ground by manual labor into baking soda. Members of the family helped fill the packages.

After Daniel came Henry A. and later Levi J. De Land, to carry on the business. Henry, a leader in church and political affairs, built the $40,000 mansion that is now the Green Lantern Inn. Later it was the residence of Victor Holmes, who called it Villa Rosenberg, after a castle he knew in Denmark.

Henry De Land left Fairport to found De Land, Fla., and to help establish Stetson University there. In 1893 a disastrous fire swept the saleratus works. The industry declined but baking soda was manufactured in Fairport up to 1928 when Dudley & Co. made the last package of the Napoleon brand, closed its doors and wrote finis to one chapter of the town's industrial story.

Since 1865 proprietary medicines have been made in a three-story building beside the railroad tracks in Main Street. Once George C. Taylor shipped his bottles all over the world. Buffalo Bill Cody ordered Taylor's Oil of Life sent to him in Manchester, England.

Dr. Weare made condition powders for domestic animals and the Fairport Crystal Rock Water Co. briefly shipped out mineral water, procured from the Peddie Spring in the 1880's. Verily Fairport's products have been varied and unusual.

* * * *

The canal town had its day as a canning center, too. The Edgetts, pioneer canners, began the industry in Fairport in 1872 but it was the Cobbs, the "canning clan," Amos H. and his four sons, particularly George W., that developed it at Cobb's Bridge and along with it the food container business.

In the 1880's the making of cans was a laborious process, mostly hand labor, with tinsmith's shears, soldering irons and foot presses. A press cut a hole in the top of the can, the fruit or vegetable was pushed through the hole, the cap soldered on and the filled can immersed in boiling water. If the cans did not swell and burst, they were ready for the consumer's table. If they did—the canal was handy.

The Cobbs were not satisfied with this crude process. They pioneered in the use of the solderless, double seamed can and out of their faith and perseverance there evolved the Sanitary Can Company, which was sold to the American Can combine in 1908. The huge can plant sprawls along the north side of the canal today, a major Fairport industry. But the old Cobb plant by the eastern bridge, a cradle of the canning industry, is only a storehouse.

*   *   *   *

When Robert Douglas was a boy in Scotland, working in his father's marmalade shop, he began experiments in extracting the natural pectin from fruit to save labor and expense in making jams and jellies. A Frenchman discovered the process but it was Douglas who later perfected and patented it.

In time Douglas came to America and in 1907 to Fairport, where he bought the abandoned De Land saleratus works and established a vinegar plant. This plant at one time shipped one-seventh of the world's vinegar. But all the time Douglas was working with apples to perfect the pectin process.

In 1912 Lowell Cuthbert, who is still in the laboratories of the company, now Certo, Inc., a division of the gigantic General Foods Corporation, poured the first bottle of pectin. "It was murky, it was gooey, but it worked," he recalls.

It was in the old De Land office, the frame building that faces Main Street and looks like a dwelling. In the 1890's it had been the meeting place for the Fairport Band, of which Levi De Land was the chief sponsor. The leader at one time was Robert Wagnalls Sr., who as a member of the Marine Band of England, had played at the wedding of Edward VII to Princess Alexandria.

After victory crowned the Douglas experiment, the pectin was shipped out in barrels and large tins for the wholesale trade, largely to the jam-loving British.

A half million dollar fire swept the plant in Setpember, 1921. As one fireman recalls, "vinegar was running over the firemen's boots." Most of the plant was destroyed, but the old office-laboratory was spared. Undaunted, Douglas and his associates rebuilt and began putting their product up in small bottles for the retail trade. In 1928 the business was sold to General Foods—for a matter of twenty-nine million dollars!

In his days of early struggle, Robert Douglas lived in Fairport. Later on, he removed to Rochester. His will left stock with a value of $8,000 to found the village's fine new library which was erected in 1937. A feature of the library is a striking mural depicting the town's history, done by Carl Peters, a local artist.

* * * *

Many one-time mansions of the wealthy now serve the community.

The rambling Potter homestead with wide lawns, on West Church Street, built from early telegraph company investments, has been given to the village as a community house.

The former L. J. De Land residence on the north side of town is now the central building of the Monroe County Baptist Home where elderly folk spend the twilight of their lives amid pleasant surroundings.

* * * *

After the Ditch crosses the Irondequoit Valley on the Great Embankment, it makes a sweeping swing to the north. The curve has been known from time immemorial as the Ox-Bow. The Barge Canal made it a widewaters and today, amid the cattails, clusters a colony of some 50 year-round homes on land leased from the state. In other days, Fairporters skated, swam, fished and picnicked there.

On April 28, 1871, a 510-foot-section of the canal bank gave way at the Ox-Bow, because of a burrowing muskrat. The waters spilled over acres of land, carrying away bridges—and the canal barge, Bonnie Bird. The boat was deposited against a tree, a mile from the canal. Neither the skipper, his wife, his steersman, nor a team of horses aboard was injured. The wreck stood in a field for many a year.

The washout drained the canal level between the Pittsford and Macedon locks and boats were tied up for miles along the waterway.

Workmen were rushed in to repair the break. They were a rough, hard drinking lot. When their demand for pay in advance of the designated day was denied, they rebelled, pushed horses into the canal, raised Cain generally. The 54th Regiment was called out from Rochester to put down the insurrection. The sight of the uniforms and the guns ended the trouble. The militia stood guard for several days until the break was repaired and their stay at the Ox-Bow was enlivened by the visits of the young women of Fairport who brought them cakes and lemonade.

* * * *

Frank Scribner, 79-year-old retired shoeworker, now living in Rochester, paints a graphic word picture of the Fairport he knew in his boyhood, in the late 1870's. He was born on the canal boat of his father, Oliver Scribner, in Hoboken. When Frank was three years old, his father moved to Fairport and opened a canal grocery at the Parker Street bridge. Here are some of Frank Scribner's indelible memories of old Fairport:

The night barns his father ran opposite the grocery, barns that housed ten teams in the days before the canal boats were equipped with stables for extra horses or mules and when they had to tie up every night—the mules, the minute they were unhitched and wherever they were, rolling over and over, often into the canal—sometimes his father sold a horse to replace a drowned mule and oddly matched teams hauled boats out of Fairport—the winter that saw

17 canal boats "frozen in" and the spoon-bowed ice breakers that made a path so they could tie up to the horse bridge—the sad day when two young girls and a boy from one of the boats went skating on the thin ice of Clark's mill pond and were drowned—the Chadwick warehouse bulging with produce—sometimes 15 boats loading at the docks—the cooperage shops, the wagon factories, the great tiers of apple barrels, the potatoes shipped loose in the barges, lined with lath and packed in straw—the New York buyers arriving in the fall—the old Osburn House between the tracks, the leading hostelry of its day and the farmers leaving their horses in its barn while they took the train to the city—that was Fairport in the 1870's.

* * * *

Old timers will remember Marion S. (Cap) Kelsey, for fifty years a canal boatman, and the owner of steam freight packets and excursion boats. He resides in Rochester now but during his canal days lived in Fairport, one of the six Kelsey brothers. Marion and S. Roy followed the canal.

Among the Kelsey boats were the Whipple, the M. P. Brown, the Ruth and the William B. Kirk. They carried many an excursion in the halcyon 90's before the motor age. Their names evoke memories of moonlight excursions and of young voices blending in old refrains; of sedate Sunday-school picnics to Ayrault's Woods, east of Fairport, where the spring water was so cool; of noisier parties where no water was drunk; of the Fairport ball team and firemen visiting Palmyra and the other canal towns by boat—while the band played on.

There were the other boats owned by Fairporters—the Jessie, captained by Ed Hurlbert and later by Henry Van Wagenen; D. O. Worden's speedy Wanderer; H. H. Buckley's Dora; the Rambler, that transported cannery employes to Fairport from other canal towns in the busy season; the private yachts of the De Lands and the Cobbs. Now they are all gone; sunk, burned, rotted and rusted away and there remain as "Cap" Kelsey sadly put it, "only the memories of the good old days."

* * * *

Charles Joseph (Joe) Bieler is probably the world's oldest trapper. Little Joe will tell you he is 96 years old and that this winter, as he has for 80 years, he will run his line of traps again to Shortsville, 20 miles away. Joe works in his garden from dawn to dusk in the summertime and boasts "There ain't a weed in it." Joe has served as constable and because he bought cherries once for a cannery, he has been called "The Cherry King."

A few years ago he was run down by a car and people thought Joe would never recover. He was back in his garden in a few months. A Fairport artist, Mrs. Carmen Peck, has painted Joe Bieler, coming down the road with his hoe over his shoulder, a wisp-like but indomitable figure.

* * * *

Probably Fairport's most exciting time was the night of Oct. 20, 1920. The affray has been mistakenly called "The Fairport Riot." It was no riot. It was a village defending itself against armed invasion.

The Saturday night before there had been a fight over a girl between visiting Rochesterians and local youths at a dance in the Town Hall. The city gang vowed revenge. Five nights later, six auto loads invaded the peaceful village. Each wore a handkerchief on his wrist for identification. They were armed with clubs, ice picks, bottles and ax handles. They were known to city police as "The Central Avenue gang."

The villagers, warned of the invasion, halted the cavalcade on the main street, gave battle and routed the Rochesterians. Fairporters grabbed guns and every other kind of weapon. East Rochester and Pittsford men poured in to join the battle. A riot call went out and police cars sped to the scene.

The unwelcome visitors returned. Gun fire crackled in the crowded street, and a Negro youth, one of the invading party, was killed. Soon Fairport had routed the second invasion. Sixteen Rochesterians were rounded up and arrested. There was an exciting trial and a half dozen men served time in the "Pen." The incident is well remembered, after 25 years, both in the city and the village.

Before I left Fairport, I took another look at the lift bridge that straddles the canal at Main Street. It probably is the most unusual one along the Ditch. It is not only built on a slant but also "cut on the bias," so that when it is up, it shuts off traffic on two streets, Main and West Avenue.

I spotted a little state tug, tied up east of the bridge. It is used in dredging operations up around Wayneport. I glanced at the name on its side. It was THE DE WITT CLINTON.

I had a chat with the captain, corpulent, good humored Austin "Snub" Huftill of Waterford. He's been on the canal for 64 years, ever since he was a boy of two. He puffed away on his pipe and talked of other, livelier times.

"There's too much talk about fights and rough times on the canal," he observed. "Those stories are exaggerated. I'd rather raise children on a canal boat than in a town."

The captain was mighty convincing. But I still think there may have been a fight or two on the old Towpath.

"Snub" Huftill knows every canal town from Buffalo to Albany.

"Fairport? A good town. Just the same as it always was."

And that's a canaller's accolade!

The Erie's Last Stand

WHO said the old Erie Canal is only a memory, and gone forever from the scene? I'm afraid I did—much earlier in these pages. But that was before I had been to Macedon.

There "Erie water" is not merely a romantic phrase. At Macedon there's water in the old Erie and the ditch is still navigable—for small craft. I saw a pleasure boat, a "putt-putter," moored on the shore of the authentic Erie water in the canal town that bears the name of an ancient Grecian state.

The sepia-colored current rolls for some three miles through the channel that was dug a century ago. To the north is the broader, newer Barge Canal. To the south linger traces of the first Clinton Ditch. Macedonians speak of the "three canals" as if they were separate waterways.

Eerie water flows through the Erie ditch. Ghosts trudge along the old Towpath, shades of the blasphemous "hoggies" and the patient mules they drove. And out of the past come the booming voices of the captains, as their boats near the locks of Macedon:

*"Who-o-a, Johnny. Who-o-a, Johnny.
Keep your lines slack."*

Phantom craft ride the narrow current. There are log rafts,

steam packets, excursion boats, the Green Fleet with its rich cargo of Western grain, the ale boat out of Syracuse.

The Towpath, following a trail of memory, winds through a mystical countryside. In this county, named after "Mad Anthony" Wayne, strange shadows fall, shadows of the drumlins, those knobby hillocks, some of them fantastic in shape, that are relics of the Glacial Age when the great ice sheet covered the land.

It is the realm of the "isms," too. Here among the drumlins, mystical new cults took strong root in frontier soil. Two of them lived to spread their doctrines throughout the world. But that is another story to be told in other chapters.

Maybe it is because the Erie water has lingered longest at Macedon that memories of the old canal are so vivid there. Maybe it is because Macedon was a "two-lock" town and smaller than her neighboring ports, and as a consequence the old ditch was of greater significance in her community life that the canal tradition is so enduring there.

And of course there are the tangible remnants, possessed by few other ports, the murky waters still flowing in the Erie; the masonry of the old locks east of the village, still sturdy, still defying the years and the elements.

* * * *

The Clinton Ditch made Macedon. In 1823, two years before the waterway was completed across the state, the township was set apart from Palmyra and that same year saw Wayne County created and named in honor of the "blood and guts" general of the Revolution.

The first settlement in the town was as early as 1789. The dawn of the 19th Century found a little colony at the crossroads at the present western limits of the village. It was called "The Huddle."

To the north was Macedon Center, with its Quaker pioneers. The old academy founded by the Society of Friends and the second Quaker meeting house still stand in the hamlet that the railroads and the canal skipped.

When the canal was dug, settlement gravitated to the two locks, only a mile apart, and "The Huddle" moved eastward. For years the village was called Macedon Locks. The 17-mile lockless level that began at Pittsford ended there. Now Macedon is a one-lock town with modern No. 30 on the Barge Canal not far from the old hand-operated western Erie locks.

* * * *

For years travelers on New York Central limiteds have gazed out at the great, gaunt trestles and tanks at Wayneport and wondered why so important a train was stopping in "the wilderness."

For years Wayneport was THE coaling and water station on the Main Line, and proud trains that flashed by far bigger places all halted there. Nowadays water is caught "on the fly" and the Diesel powered locomotives that haul such trains as the Century no longer need to stop at Wayneport. But the freights do.

The Barge Canal attains noble proportions there, resembling a mighty river. There are a few cottages along the banks. From a bridge at the tiny village one can see the Erie ditch flowing quietly beside its more pretentious successor. The Erie water that begins there rejoins the Barge east of Macedon.

In the little cemetery north of Wayneport rest the bones of 26 laborers who died of the smallpox while they were building the Clinton Ditch.

And it was to Wayneport that in 1825 40 yoke of oxen hauled the canal boat that Sutherland Pattison had built beside his Red Mill at Farmington, the Quaker village three miles to the southward.

Only this year flames devoured the 132-year-old mill, on the property of historically-minded Lewis F. Allen, whose grandfather came there by canal packet in 1848.

*   *   *   *

The first Macedonians were from New England. But with the canal and the railroads came the Irish and many of them stayed to found families in the village. Macedon is in the center of a fertile farm belt. Swamps have been transformed into rich mucklands. Dairying is carried on extensively on the farms among the drumlins.

Once Macedon had an industry that for nearly 60 years was its commercial backbone. In 1849 Bickford & Huffman, who had started business in a smithy at the "Huddle," began making by hand the first successful grain drill in America. Earlier ones were clumsy affairs, releasing an uneven flow of seed. The Macedon product, known the world over as "The Farmer's Favorite," had fertilizer and grass seed attachments and was a boon to farmers everywhere.

Before the Civil War, the South was the best customer. The war ended that, but the drill plant flourished and shipped its products to such far places as New Zealand and Australia. The Macedon Agricultural Works' trade mark was two sheaves of wheat, with the Biblical slogan: "As ye sow, so also shall ye reap."

It was a bitter day for Macedon when the drill company was sold in 1905 to a big combination and moved to Springfield, Ohio. Its importance to the canal town may be gauged by the fact that in its heyday it employed nearly 300 hands and that the present population of Macedon, according to the federal nose count of 1940, was 557.

One of the old factory buildings still stands on the main street. Macedon's principal industry today is the Grange League Federation food plant at the eastern rim of the village. It stands squarely over the first lock of the Clinton Ditch.

* * * *

I had a friend in Rochester who was born and spent his boyhood in Macedon. Clute Noxon, for years connected wtih a city brokerage firm, all his life cherished a sentimental attachment for his home town.

He was an able writer, particularly expert in yachting matters. In his later years, as a hobby, he was writing his recollections of his boyhood in the "two-lock town". One day last spring, he pressed a manuscript into my hand, saying, "Some things I remember about the old canal." Three days later my friend was dead, struck down by a truck in downtown Rochester.

I am going to share with you some of Clute's entertaining lore of the old Erie. He wrote about how in pre-game law days the spring brought out the anglers with their nets to the waterway. "The nets were big enough to reach across the canal and when hauled in, they contained about every specimen of piscatorial life known to fresh water."

Clute Noxon recalled those lively long-gone winters when a dozen canal boats were "frozen in" at Macedon Locks and the canal folk made up a colony, called the Erie Social Club, which held many parties in which the villagers joined. There always was an entente cordiale between the canal folk and the Macedonians, stronger than in other ports. But the term, canal folk, did not include "hoggies."

Sundays in the 1880's the Macedonians would saunter to the locks to see the boats go through, just as in railroad towns the populace would turn out en masse for the 5:45. Sometimes they would help the locktenders pull the heavy gates. As for the boys, "we would run around like Huck Finns all week but come Sunday we were little Lord Fauntleroys to the last curl and buckle. So when we presented ourselves to the boat captains, we stood a better chance of getting a ride between the locks on that day."

And there were the canal groceries, redolent of herring and with horse collars hanging from the ceiling. "The one at the upper lock had a huge vat sunk deep into the earth into which was piped cold, clear water from a hillside spring. Boatmen, always on the lookout for good drinking water, came to know this Pierian port well."

There was one unscrupulous grocer who weighed the meat hook with the salt pork and whose counter was overlaid with oil cloth. "About midway in the oil cloth he cut a slit, so ingeniously that it was invisible. When a boatman laid out a ten spot to pay for some $4 worth of goods, the grocer always managed to have plenty of silver among his change.

"Then counting it out slowly and carefully but taking care to lay it down on his side of the slit, he would say with a flourish as he shoved the pile across the counter: 'There you are, sir. Have a cigar and thank you.' The captain, elated with the cigar, would scoop up the change and go aboard, not knowing that anywhere from $1.50 to $2.50 reposed in the little cotton upholstered till.

"One captain had been victimized several times, finally detected the fraud and changed the name of his boat, substituting the grocer's name. For a middle initial he had painted the fattest hog that space would permit. This traveling advertisement was too much for the crooked merchant and he soon left for parts unknown."

Clute recalled that "outside of fires, elections and rounding up of hoboes, the most thrilling episodes in the town's life were when the timber craft put in an appearance at the locks. They were the bane of the locktender's existence and anathema to the other boat men.

"From 100 to 200 feet long, they crawled along under mule power. At a lock the tow had to be broken into sections and after being dropped to the lower level, reassembled. As there were five or six sections, locktenders would be on the jump for hours and traffic tied up either way. When the log rafts came, seven up and stud poker ended in the shanties at the locks.

"As fast as the tenders could get the contraption through, by way of farewell and good riddance, they would throw the paddles wide open, producing a current that would scatter the sections and leave them drifting far apart. The raftmen would pole around trying to collect their disjointed craft, yelling imprecations while the other boaters howled in unholy glee.

"It was a great show while it lasted and the villagers, whenever they heard a raft was going through, made a bee line for the locks."

I have quoted liberally from Clute Noxon's manuscript because I think he has preserved a rare bit of Americana and if I may be pardoned a little personal sentiment, because I want to pay my humble tribute to the memory of a fine gentleman and my good friend.

*   *   *   *

In Macedon I sought out Carl Gates, the watchmaker, who has spent most of his 80 years in the village. Physical infirmities keep him confined to his home nowadays but his memory roves far back into Towpath days.

He recalled lively times when the boats were tied up at Macedon by breaks in the canal banks and the "hoggies," roamed at large, doing a bit of pillaging, while the other more substantial boatmen got temporary jobs in the town. Carl Gates told of the old groceries at the locks, John McCann's and Henry Ripley's among them; of the red Breese warehouse that still squats on the Erie bank and which held such huge stores of apples and potatoes in bygone autumns.

The old gentleman called to mind boyhood days when three blasts of a steam packet's whistle brought youngsters on a run to the locks, maybe to catch a glimpse of, and may be a ride on, such fascinating vessels as the Annie Laurie, the Advance or the ale boat from Syracuse.

*   *   *   *

Down at Palmyra, I chatted with big, 73-year-old William H. Cator, a life long resident of Macedon until his recent removal to the larger eastern village. For many years he ran the Macedon Hotel that burned down some years ago. His father was a lock tender on the old ditch and Will Cator briefly served as a deckhand on a scow that transported corn from Macedon to the Cobb cannery at Fairport.

"We had to pump her out all the time to keep her afloat. Later that old scow sank," and Cator chuckled as he said it.

In Macedon near Erie water lives John Cook, who has Indian blood in his veins and who is a helper around Lock 30 and keeps the grounds so spick and span. He showed me where the circus boats used to dock and where they pitched their tents. Oaken snubbing posts are still visible along the ditch. Cook remembered when Governor Theodore Roosevelt, then the youngish hero of San Juan Hill, came through by canal boat on an inspection trip in 1899.

Tall, silver-haired Mark Harrington and his blue mariner's cap are inseparable. His father once drove mules on the old Towpath. Mark and his wife, the daughter of John Hamilton, a boatman, have many memories of the horse and mule days, of the excursion boats, of riding bicycles on the Towpath. Mrs. Harrington told of going out in a rowboat to sell produce to the canallers who sometimes tossed back the pay, stuck in a potato.

For 51 years Dr. Cyrus P. Jennings has practiced medicine in the canal town and with a keen and kindly eye watched the changing scene. He is still in harness. Among his thousands of patients through the years have been occasional canallers. A few years ago a middle-aged woman came to his door, announcing that he had brought her into the world in 1896—on a canal boat. The doctor recalled the incident and the neat home-like cabin of the boat.

Macedon well remembers another physician, Dr. Edwin M. Rodenberger, who died a year ago after practising for 55 years in the village. On July 3, 1936 Macedon was the scene of a gala christening, when the 38 foot cabin cruiser that the doctor had spent seven years in building, slid down into Erie water. The doctor was then 76 and had put all his leisure time in the building of his boat, aided by his daughter, Beth. For many happy summers he sailed the canal and Great Lake waters.

*   *   *   *

I think the typical "Canal Town" is Macedon, the old "two-lock town," in the shadow of the drumlins, by the River Ganargua that some call Mud Creek, beside the eternal Erie water.

The Grand Dame

DOWN Macedon way, I heard Palmyra referred to as "Pal." It seemed almost sacrilege, like calling Plymouth Rock "Plym" or Bunker Hill "Bunk."

No diminutive fits so stately, so distinctive a village as 156-year-old Palmyra, the Grand Dame of the Towpath.

Samuel Hopkins Adams made the Wayne County village the symbolic "Canal Town" of his novel of that name. But Palmyra is much more than just "Canal Town." The canal is only an incident in her compelling history.

It was the spring-fed Ganargua River and no man-made ditch that brought the first settlers to the drumlin land. De Witt Clinton's name is not on her certificate of birth. He was an unknown stripling of 20 when the town was born. Palmyra was an up and coming frontier settlement long before the Clinton Ditch was dug. A decade before the canal came, her broad main street was the drill ground for the militia in the War of 1812.

Palmyra, named after a city in ancient Syria, is drenched in history and glitters with the glamor of great names.

It was there that an obscure and unlettered farm youth named Joseph Smith dreamed a wondrous dream of golden plates hidden in a drumlin's breast. Out of that vision sprang a powerful church.

Today a towering white shaft on the Sacred Hill Cumorah marks a world shrine for thousands of the Mormon faith.

The blood of Palmyra pioneers throbs in the stout heart of Winston Churchill, that grand old warrior who rallied England in her darkest hour—when she stood alone and the fate of civilization trembled in the balance.

On a side street under the brow of Prospect Hill stands the buff and brown house where 105 years ago William T. Sampson was born. That Palmyra boy became the famous admiral of the War with Spain and today a huge naval center on Seneca Lake that trained tens of thousands of Bluejackets for World War II bears his name.

Years ago another youth began his career in Palmyra, carrying parcels in a paper bag, on foot. His name was Henry Wells and he became the co-founder of the Wells-Fargo Express Company that carried tons of parcels to the ends of the earth.

Do you think a town with such traditions should be called "Pal"?

* * * *

Palmyra is a breath from the long ago. More than 100 of her buildings are at least a century old. Historic inns, stone warehouses and gray old buildings along the Towpath, tasteful, substantial, mellow brick residences, Colonial homes with pillars, fan windows, old fashioned blinds and classical doorways tell even the casual visitor that this is no "Johnny Come Lately" town.

Palmyra has a Canandaigua-like air, a flavor of New England, with a touch of the Hudson Valley and a dash of the Old South, too. The mixture is altogether charming and spells an antiquarian's paradise.

But despite her stateliness and her aura of great age, Palmyra is a factory town—with none of the usual attributes. She is a one-factory town and the Garlock plant, largest manufacturer of steam packing in the world, stretches along the railroad tracks, a respectful distance from the historic homes.

The industry draws its labor from all over the region. For Palmyra's official population is 2,709 and the Garlock plant has 1,600 employes. Incidentally, Palmyra's population is nearly 100 per cent native American.

*   *   *   *

Ganargua means "where the village sprang up" in the Indian tongue. And it was beside the narrow river (also known as plain Mud Creek) that Palmyra had its beginnings.

The Ganargua undergoes several transitions in its journey from the Bristol Hills to Three Rivers, where it joins the Oswego River. Around Palmyra it now is a part of the Barge Canal, thereby eliminating an oldtime flood hazard. At Lyons where it unites with the outlet of Canandaigua Lake, it becomes the Clyde River and later, the Seneca.

The surveyors, John Swift and John Jenkins, came from Pennsylvania's Wyoming Valley to the region in March of 1789. They reared a shanty, the first habitation of white man in the neighborhood. The next year Swift returned and built the first covered log house along the Ganargua at the eastern edge of the present village.

The tall, soldierly figure of John Swift dominated the pioneer scene. He was the first citizen in every sense of the word, influential in business, in politics and in war. He built mills at what is now Main and Canal Streets and the settlement was first known as Swift's Landing or Swift Town. Later for a brief time it was called Tolland.

When the war clouds darkened the frontier in 1812, Swift, a veteran of the Revolution, drilled the raw militia on the main street.

He became a general and fell at the battle of Queenstown Heights in Canada, treacherously shot down by a British prisoner of war.

He sleeps, with other pioneers, in the old burying ground on an eminence that overlooks the canal. The American Legion post keeps the historic cemetery in shape.

*   *   *   *

After Swift, other settlers came in boats up the Ganargua, to dwell on the creek bottoms east of the present village. A colony of Rhode Islanders arrived in 1791 and ten families of Long Islanders the next year. Among the Rhode Islanders were the Durfees, who planted the first apple seeds and Weaver Osband who developed the Osband pear. Another was David Wilcox, the great grandfather of Winston Churchill.

Some of the pioneers, following a trail of fresh horse prints, came upon a cabin in the thick woods. Its occupant, probably the first white man in those parts, was clad in rough clothes. But he was a man of obvious breeding. Skins about the place told his occupation. He had hunted and trapped there for nine years with no near neighbors save the Indians.

"William Fleming is my name," he said in a cultivated English voice. Then to the amazement of the settlers, he began quoting verse:

> "I wish I were a hunter in some strange and savage land,
> The lasso by my saddle bow, the rifle in my hand;
> With a leash of gallant mastiffs bounding by my side,
> And no friend to love me but the gallant horse I ride."

Shortly William Fleming vanished. The country was becoming too settled for him. Doubtless he sought some new "strange and savage land."

The pioneers erected a blockhouse in 1794 on Wintergreen Hill when fears of an Indian uprising alerted the thinly populated frontier. Wayne's victory in Ohio ended that threat.

The Durfees entertained a royal visitor in 1796 when Louis Philippe, later a king of France, stopped on his tour of the backwoods.

The next year the name of the town was changed to Palmyra because, so the story goes, Daniel Sawyer wanted to impress his schoolteacher sweetheart with his knowledge of ancient history.

* * * *

By 1812 Palmyra was a considerable settlement with a tavern, a church, a distillery, several stores, mills and shops. It also had two schools, one for children of Federalists, the other for the Republicans, so bitter was the political feeling of the time.

Then the canal came and things began to hum. The pioneer packet boat, the Myron Holley, was built at Palmyra. So was the Twin Brothers, named after its owners, John and Levi Thayer.

But tides of history other than the backwash of Erie water were surging across the land of the drumlins.

* * * *

Palmyra is widely known as the birthplace of Mormonism although the hill of its nativity is just over the line in Manchester, Ontario County.

In 1816 Joseph Smith Sr. came to Palmyra from Royalton, Vt. with his wife, six sons and three daughters. The third son, a towhead, was Joseph Jr. Early Wayne County historians were not kind to the Smiths. "Shifty and shiftless" are among the milder adjectives applied to them.

For two and one-half years the family lived in the village where the father peddled gingerbread and root beer in a hand cart.

In 1818 they moved to a farm south of Palmyra. There Joseph had his vision. Today that farm is owned by the Mormon Church.

The rest is familiar history; the "discovery" of the golden plates with their revelations in 1827 and the printing of the Mormon Bible in Palmyra three years later. That same year saw the hegira of the faithful westward under Smith; first to Kirtland, Ohio, and then to Nauvoo, Ill., where the leader was killed by a mob. Brigham Young, the bearded former Mendon glazier and stone mason, took over the command and led his people across the desert and the mountains to found a virtual empire beside the Great Salt Lake.

Of the Mormon host that followed Smith westward, only thirty came from the Palmyra locality and once when Sidney Rigdon, the Mormon preacher, sought recruits at a rally in the village, his audience was small and unsympathetic.

Is there not an old adage about a prophet and his own country?

Despite Joseph Smith's background and obvious faults, this farm lad who founded a mighty church must have possessed qualities of leadership and magnetism.

*   *   *   *

Now the magic hill of his dreams is a shrine of the church and each summer a pageant of impressive beauty is held at the towering monument. And the old Canandaigua road is clogged with automobiles, many bearing Utah license plates.

During Pliny T. Sexton's lifetime, he would not sell the Mormon Hill property to the sect although he allowed the Mormons to visit their sacred ground at will. On Sexton's death, the property was sold to the church with the proviso that the Latter Day Saints buy also the former Grange Hall in Cuyler Street, Palmyra. It still is their church and services are held there regularly.

For nearly 40 years now the Mormons have maintained a colony of some 75 to 100 members at the Sacred Hill and the Smith

Farm. They are a carefully selected group, mainly from the mother church, and each serves about five years. Among them are missionaries. The Mormon children attend the village schools. Some of them are outstanding athletes and students. Elder Willard Beam, who headed the first contingent and who remained as leader in the area for 25 years, won a high place in the esteem of tolerant Palmyra and at one time was president of the village Lions Club.

* * * *

Remember one David Wilcox among the Rhode Islanders who came to the green valley in 1791? He had a comely daughter, Clarissa. One day around 1820 she went to the door to give a drink of water to a thirsty hunter from Massachusetts named Ambrose Hall. It was love at first sight. Hall came back the next year, to stay and to marry Clarissa Wilcox. For years they lived in the village on the approximate site of the bandstand in the park.

They had six daughters. One of them, Clarissa, married Leonard Jerome. Another, Caroline, married Leonard's brother, Lawrence. The Jeromes were prosperous young farmers who had come from Pompey in Onondaga County to live on a farm north west of Marion. They were dashing, handsome chaps with a liking for good horseflesh. The old Jerome place is still standing.

The Jerome brothers did not stay long at farming. They moved to Rochester, then to New York, where they amassed wealth. Leonard became a publisher, a patron of the arts, a race track owner, a diplomat and a world traveler. One of his four daughters was Jenny Jerome, a dark-haired beauty. Jenny met a titled Englishman, Lord Randolph Churchill, at a ball on the moonlight-bathed deck of a British man of war. He danced with her again and again. They fell deeply in love and married despite some parental objections.

To the son of the Duke of Marlborough and the granddaughter of Ambrose Hall, the thirsty backwoods hunter, a son was born, whom they named Winston Leonard Spencer Churchill.

The Lawrence Jeromes, by the way, had a son who was much in the headlines around the turn of the century, William Travers Jerome, the colorful district attorney of New York.

The little office in Palmyra's Market Street, where Lady Churchill's uncle, Hiram K. Jerome, practiced law, has only recently been torn down and old timers remember hearing their fathers and mothers tell of visits Jenny Jerome as a girl paid to her Palmyra kin.

Winston Churchill has one trait that is decidedly un-English—a streak of audacity. Perhaps that is a heritage from his ancestors who were pioneers in Wayne County, New York, and from the American grandfather who was wont to take bold chances in the stock market and at the race track.

* * * *

It was more than a century ago that Henry Wells began carrying parcels around Palmyra on foot. Soon he made enough to buy a horse and wagon. Then he married a Palmyra lass, Sally Daggett. In 1845 he formed the express agency of Wells and Company and later joined forces with Henry Fargo. Again the rest of the Horatio Alger tale is history.

* * * *

In 1840 William Thomas Sampson was born in the old house at Vienna and Johnson Streets of sturdy Scotch Presbyterian stock. A slim, shy, industrious boy, he trudged to the little stone schoolhouse on Throop Street, did odd jobs, helped his father in the garden, was an ordinary village lad of his time and circumstances. When he was 17 he won appointment to the Naval Academy at Annapolis.

Right after his graduation, the Civil War broke out and Will Sampson became a midshipman on a frigate. Thereafter his climb up the ladder was steady and sure. He became a recognized authority on tactics and technical problems so that when Uncle Sam declared war on Spain, Sampson was given command of the North Atlantic Squadron with the title of rear admiral.

When the fleets joined battle in Santiago Harbor, Sampson chanced to be eight miles away on his flagship, bound for a conference with General Shafter. Winfield S. Schley took charge in Sampson's absence. The American fleet scored a smashing victory and there ensued a long controversy as to whether the credit belonged to Sampson or to Schley. In the end it was conceded that the battle followed the carefully laid plans of Sampson even if he were not present to direct it.

In 1899, bearded, aging Will Sampson returned for a visit to the town where he had been born, spent his boyhood and courted his first wife, Margaret Aldrich. Palmyra gave him a hero's welcome, with an arch over Main Street, flags, music, parades and oratory.

The admiral died in Washington in 1902. The following year the Navy Department sent to Palmyra the 14 centimeter gun that Sampson's fleet had captured from a Spanish man of war. It stands silent sentinel in the village park today.

It is recalled that the gun came to town on a flat car and was hauled from the railroad station, a mile away, to the village, by a threshing machine.

* * * *

A distinguished Palmyran, who stayed in Palmyra, was the late Pliny T. Sexton, son of a sturdy Quaker father who in 1827 built the old brick house on Main Street. A blue marker there tells that it once was a station of the Underground Railway. Pliny, the younger, became a lawyer, a banker, a chancellor of the state Regents, and the village's benefactor.

He gave Palmyra Sexton Park, the twenty-acre wooded picnic spot on the hill south of town. He also gave the Union Club, still a center of communal activities, and the adjacent park on Main Street. Sexton believed all civic groups should be merged into a Union Club. He provided the meeting place and when the rooms were outgrown, motion pictures were shown twice a week in winter in the old Opera House and in summers, crowds in the park watched the screen on the brick wall of the Union Club.

* * * *

Palmyra owes much industrially to Olin J. Garlock, who in the early 1880's, cut up a piece of fire hose to stop the leak in the stuffing box of the steam engine he was tending in a little saw mill at Port Gibson. He made rings of the hose, then after soaking them in oil, put them in the box. They stopped the leak and needed no replacing for many days.

The first packing for commercial use was cooked in a kettle and was made of duck and rubber belting. Out of that grew the great steam packing industry.

Palmyra has had other industries among them two plants that made printing presses and rival packing factories.

There also was a rope factory, called a "rope walk," which in the 1850's, when the New York Central was built, made a giant rope 2,000 feet long to haul the engines up hill in Albany.

* * * *

State Senator Henry W. Griffith, whose father, Frederick W., also was a senator and a member of the triumvirate that built the Garlock industry, took me on a tour of Palmyra with an eye to canal lore.

We saw the "cross-over bridge" that once carried the Towpath from one side of the Ditch to the other and that now spans the Ganargua, west of the village. It has a circular rail on one side so that the tow rope would slide over it without catching.

We visited the old "Aqueduct," where the modern locks now stand and where the stocky, chain-smoking, likeable senator said he learned to swim. He called to mind the night of July 3, 1929, when heavy rains undermined the power house there and left it tilted at a crazy angle. The boys of the village, celebrating the eve of the Fourth, had been tipping over sundry outbuildings that night and when the superintendent of maintenance saw the power house upset, he exclaimed: "What will those young hellions do next?"

Senator Griffith showed me the remnants of the locks of the first Clinton Ditch, in a pasture east of town. One can see evidence there of the three canals, side by side. To reach the spot, we had to crawl through a barbed wire fence. The Senator did it much more gracefully than I, despite our almost equal age and my early training in such matters.

* * * *

Dominating the Main Street scene is a steel pole that is 150 feet high. It is a Republican pole and it rose in 1892 during the second Cleveland-Harrison campaign. The Democrats raised a wooden pole that same year. They won the election but their pole did not last. The GOP pole raising was a great occasion. Marching clubs and bands came from nearby communities.

I don't think any village has a higher pole and few have so wide a main street, Canandaigua and Newark excepted.

"Believe It or Not" Ripley has taken due cognizance of the four churches, one at each corner of the intersection of Main, Church and Canandaigua Streets. It is said there's no four corners like it in the nation.

* * * *

Lanky, jovial 82-year-old Edward W. Tappenden, a resident of Palmyra since he was 10 days old, has many a tale of Towpath days. "Tapp" spoke of Franklin Lakey's warehouse where some 70 years ago everything was sold "from a rat pelt to a yoke of oxen," Lakey also operated a tannery, a silk factory and a distillery. Whisky was $1 a gallon in those days. He also dealt in cattle, sheep and hogs and Irishmen tended them in the barns along the canal. Sheep hides once were worth more than mutton and half a sheep could be purchased for 25 cents.

"Tapp" recalled the lurid days when there were 32 saloons in the village, most of them on Market and Canal Streets, and the old toll house, only recently razed, was a busy place.

* * * *

There is the tale of the inebriate, a well known villager of the time, who, in his cups, visited a livery stable and ordered a special equipage to take him home. He demanded and obtained a team of splendid black horses hitched to a hearse with nodding black plumes. Thus he rode in state up Main Street to his home—stretched out luxuriously in the carriage of his desire.

* * * *

Other landmarks of Palmyra: The fair which just closed its 90th annual showing with Governor Dewey a guest of honor. A genuine country fair, it has entertained generations of Western New Yorkers, surviving wars, rationing and the changing customs that killed off so many others. And mind you, it is not the Wayne County Fair. It is and always has been the Palmyra Fair . . . Cannon Hill on the west side where the guns boomed out the tidings that the Grand Canal was open in 1825 . . . the 111-year-old hotel beside the tall steel pole. It has been variously known as the Eagle Tavern, the Nottingham, the Powers and the Palmyra. Once the massive pillars extended down to the street level and once some poker classics were staged there. The old yellow brick inn to the east, now known as Sellen's and once also called the Eagle, also is of great antiquity . . . There's the square, lemon-colored Carleton Rogers mansion on Cuyler Street, housing the rare documents and volumes of the Historical Society, presided over by Mrs. C. J. Ziegler. It was there that Samuel Hopkins Adams obtained much of the historical background for his "Canal Town." On the wide lawn are many unusual trees, including a "Tree of Heaven" from the Orient.

* * * *

Palmyra carries her many years with grace and with the dignity befitting a Grand Dame. She is pardonably proud of her heritage of tradition. Few villages have so rich a background.

She is not haughty. At heart she is downright friendly. In Palmyra villagers, youngsters among them, speak cordially to the stranger on their streets, the stranger they have never seen before.

I think it is a gracious custom and worthy of emulation.

So maybe it's all right, after all, to call the Grand Dame "Pal" —if you say it with affection and a note of reverence.

Of Rappings and of Roses

"NEWARK is one of the most pleasant and flourishing villages upon the Erie Canal. It . . . is a place of manufacturing enterprise, has a population of 1,700 and commands the trade of a wealthy agricultural community."

Turner wrote those words in 1852 in his History of the Phelps and Gorham Purchase. Change the population figures to 9,646, underscore the word "flourishing" and the description holds good today.

Newark was the most populous, busiest, most virile village I encountered in my 1945 prowl along the old Towpath. Although officially it's a village, it really is a dynamic little city—and is laid out like one.

When I visited Palmyra, the stately 156-year-old neighbor that I like to call the Grand Dame because of her wealth of tradition, a well bred voice of the old regime there dismissed upstart Newark with:

"Busy, yes, but then Newark is a new town."

Newark's answer to that would be a shrug of strong and shapely shoulders and a blithe "I should worry." At that she is not so new. She is the exact age of the Clinton Ditch that has flowed through her heart for 123 years and that nourished her in the formative years.

Traditions of bygone glory don't count much in the Newark scheme of things. She is pretty busy, thank you, minding her own business. And she has such a lot of business to mind, so many things to make and grow and sell, so much new business to go after. Buoyant Miss Newark is frankly "on the make." Her eyes ever on the future, she will march sure-footedly through the new Atomic Age.

Even as in 1852, Newark today "is a place of manufacturing enterprise." She produces, among other things, canned goods, paper containers, furniture, shrubs and nursery plants. Her mail order business is stupendous. Newark's Post Office handles annually a volume of mail equal to that of a city of 50,000.

And let it be remembered that Newark is America's "Rose Capital," boasting the largest field of growing roses in the world.

Newark annually exports whole forests of trees and enough flowers to fill the gardens of eight states. Evergreens, shade trees, shrubs, fruit trees are shipped by the thousands to all points of the compass. Every day is Arbor Day in Newark, N. Y.

Today, as in 1852, Newark "commands the trade of a wealthy agricultural community." That has always been the keystone of her commercial arch. She is in the heart of one of America's most fecund countrysides, abounding in rich mucklands and orchards, as well as nurseries. Not for nothing did the pioneers name this township Arcadia.

Newark is a trading center for 52,000 people and the hum of her busy marketplace almost drowns out the voices of the past.

I say almost—for still heard around the world are voices, not of this earth, strange rappings on the walls of a little house on Newark's outskirts that first were heard in 1848. Those supernatural knockings gave birth to the great Spiritualist Church, twenty years after the equally fantastic beginnings of Mormonism on a Palmyra hillside.

You think it strange that in such a practical, earthy town the voices "from beyond the grave" were first heard. Remember that Newark lies in the shadow of the drumlins, in the mystical land of the 'isms.

Despite her concentration on trade and material matters, she is no ugly, grimy factory town. Newark is neat and orderly and her streets are wide and shady. Although her population is of many bloods, she has no slums. She has few pretentious mansions but many homelike homes.

All in all, she's a smiling, wholesome sort of lass, this sprightly Mistress Newark, with her market basket o'er her arm and rosebuds in her hair.

*   *   *   *

It was no idyllic Arcadian land the first settlers cleared in 1791, but a tangle of woods and fever-laden swamp along the Ganargua River. In 1806 the three Lusk brothers bought a mile-square tract that included the present site of Newark. Neighbors were few and far between and the wolves howled in the dark forests. But the settlers planted seeds, cleared the marshes, hacked down the trees and waited for a better day.

That day dawned with the coming of the Grand Canal. The father of Newark was Joseph Miller, a shrewd Vermonter, who had the contract for digging $1\frac{1}{4}$ miles of the Ditch in the area. He bought 100 acres in 1819 from the Lusks, began laying out village streets and a public park and selling lots. He erected the low white house that still stands at 107 West Miller Street. He built boats in the canal basin near the present busy intersection of Union and Main streets and the booming settlement there became known as Miller's Basin.

The present Newark is a consolidation of Miller's Basin and Lockville to the east. It was named in 1838 and the origin of the name is obscure. Probably it was called after the older town in New Jersey. The Western New York Newark has always labored under the handicap of having the same name as a much larger and better known city. Besides, the situation has caused some confusion in postal circles.

Another version has the village named in honor of the English Viscount Newark, who in the early days was co-proprietor of the site under royal grant—and never saw his backwoods holdings.

From the beginning Newark was a center of trade and shipping. Produce-laden wagons from points as far distant as Sodus lined up at the busy canal docks. In pre-railroad days stages ran to Geneva. Newark's growth through the years has been steady and unspectacular. Her commercial supremacy was long challenged by the older towns of Palmyra and Lyons, but years ago they gave up the race.

*　　*　　*　　*

"Here, Mr. Splitfoot, do as I do."

It was a girlish voice that called out those fateful words on a March night in 1848, in a humble home at Hydesville, a cross-roads hamlet, 1½ miles north of Newark.

The girl, Katherine Fox, then only 12 years old, and her sister, Margaret, 14, daughters of the village blacksmith, had been hearing mysterious rappings on the walls. These goings on bothered John Fox and his wife for the region was rife with rumors that the house into which they had recently moved from Rochester, was haunted—by the ghost of a peddler who had been murdered there and buried in the cellar.

Katy Fox decided to try to converse with the invisible one. When the rappings came, she snapped her fingers a certain number of times and bade "Mr. Splitfoot" reply. The ghostly tappings answered like an echo. After that she and her sister "talked" often with the wraith. A neighbor figured out a code and from the knockings gathered the information that the spirit was that of Charles B. Rosna, the slain peddler.

Then the girls reported sounds like a heavy body being dragged down into the cellar and of feeling a clammy, icy hand. The startling news spread through the countryside. The cellar was dug up but no corpus delecti found. The roads leading to Hydesville became choked with buggies, wagons and pedestrians, bound for the scene of the uncanny rappings.. As many as 500 people flocked to the Fox home in a day.

Then the family decided to flee the haunted house and return to Rochester. A married sister, Leah Fish, took the two younger girls to the city on a canal packet. All along the way passengers kept hearing the weird tappings.

The rest of the tale is an oft-told one; how the Fox sisters gave seances and public demonstrations in Rochester's old Corinthian Hall, once to the accompaniment of mob threats; how the learned men of science debated the mystery. Most of them were skeptical but the Fox Sisters and "The Rochester Rappings" became headline news.

It was news that stirred the world and in many hearts was kindled the belief that the riddle of the ages had been solved, that at long last the stone had been rolled away from the tomb. Thousands eagerly embraced the new faith called Spiritualism that was born in a humble blacksmith's home in a drumlin-fringed valley.

In 1915 the weatherbeaten little house was moved to Lily Dale, the shrine colony of the sect. Now a plain stone marker, nearly hidden by the tall waving golden rod, beside a fallen tree at the quiet crossroads, alone marks the birthplace of modern Spiritualism.

On the stone are carved words that ring like a trumpet blast: "There is no death! There are no dead!"

*   *   *   *

Roses, as well as rappings, have spread afar the fame of Newark, N. Y.

The story of the roses began in 1873 when C. W. Stuart and his father-in-law, Albert E. Jackson, switched from their modest berry patches and sale of vegetable plants in the neighborhood to the growing of rose bushes. One of their first greenhouses was built from second hand windows obtained from a local church during a rebuilding program.

Today the Jackson-Perkins nurseries sprawl over the southwestern end of the village along Madison Street. There are two acres of experimental gardens, some 12,000 plants, 400 varieties of many hues, a riot of colorful beauty that has been viewed by thousands. The industry employs some 400 hands and maintains a herd of 300 cattle, largely for fertilizer.

Each June a two-day Festival of Roses is held in the "Rose Capital." There are parades, crowning of a Rose Queen, a grand "Moonlight and Roses" Ball and usually a visit by a celebrity.

You will find roses from Newark all over the earth. Dorothy Perkins blooms clamber over the walls of the garden of England's King at Windsor Castle.

Many of the varieties were developed by French-born Jean H. Nicolas, for 10 years head of research at Newark. He died in 1937 and his ashes rest in the gardens he loved and where he worked. In peacetime the firm sends scouts all over the world, seeking new varieties. In 1939, two weeks before Hitler blitzed into Poland, Eugene Bohrer, Nicolas' successor, sailed from Europe with several rare species.

Charles H. Perkins, president of the company, told me he had learned a bitter lesson in the naming of roses. "Political names are out," he said. "We tried the Herbert Hoover, the Neville Chamberlain, the Al Smith and the Eleanor Roosevelt. We found out there's too much political feeling."

This year's featured bloom, a rose-pink hybrid tea rose, is called the Ernie Pyle. There will be no political discord over that name.

The Jackson-Perkins shipments, combined with the huge volume of nursery goods and cosmetics that emanate from that beehive of trade on Union Street called the Commercial Building, account in a large part for Newark's tremendous post-office business. Newark's C. W. Stuart Co. is said to be the largest retail nursery firm in America.

* * * *

For 80 of his 95 years, A. Eugene Williams has lived in Newark, 72 years in the same house in High Street. When I called upon him, the old gentleman was splitting wood in the basement. Newark's oldest male resident is a broad-shouldered, rugged man who has been an elder of the Presbyterian Church for 62 years, who boasts he never drank or smoked.

Williams is a story teller of rare talent. He thunders, then lowers his voice, he pauses, he gestures, for all the world like a Shakespearean actor. Here are some of the things he told me:

"When I came to Newark from Oneida County in 1865, there were no sidewalks, no street lights. From 1870 to 1877 I worked in my father's store along the canal where the gasoline station now stands at Main and Union. Later on I ran the store. I learned something about the canal and about canallers.

"Those 1870s were rough times and because there had been an epidemic of burglaries, I slept in the store nights—on guard, revolver by my side.

"One night I awoke to hear what I thought was the rasp of a hacksaw severing the iron bars on a basement window facing the canal. I grabbed the gun, stole down on all fours, my heart pounding. I crouched behind a post, prepared to shoot it out. Then I heard the same rasping noise in a different direction and spotted the intruder. It was a big gray rat."

I wish you could have heard the old gentleman tell the story.

Williams recalled the old line barns on the Towpath where horses and mules not stabled on the boats, were quartered for the night; how the mules would roll when stripped of harness and how some captains had tan-bark strips for them to roll on.

"The mule," Williams declared, "when properly taken care of, is the healthiest, hardest-working, most faithful of all draft animals."

He talked about the locks, how the boats ganged up there. Once a captain, held up by the congestion at the locks, ordered a sizeable bill of goods for immediate delivery. Williams put up the goods, tossed them into a democrat wagon, drove rapidly down the Towpath and delivered the order seconds before the customer's boat was locked through.

Few living men have had canal boats named after them. Williams is one. A friend of his father, a Newark captain, christened one of his craft, the A. E. Williams. "As was the custom, my father presented a set of lines to the captain. It cost him a pretty penny. No, I never knew what finally became of the A. E. Williams," said the nonagenarian, a little sadly.

* * * *

Miss Clara Prescott lives in the charming white colonial house on East Miller Street in which she was born 89 years ago. She is the granddaughter of Dr. Joel Prescott, who in Canandaigua in 1792 was enjoined by law from inoculating patients against small pox. When her father, John Prescott, built the house, now in the heart of the town, friends chided him for "going so far out."

Miss Prescott has many memories of bygone days—of riding the packets as a girl, of taking visitors to the locks to see the boats go through, of seeing tobacco growing along Coulson Avenue in the 1880's. She has kept a scrap book for years. Through its pages old Newark marches in review through many decades. One name appeared in so many accounts of the business and social life of the town, drillmaster at carnivals, active in the Opera Club. That was C. P. H. Vary, still a part of the Newark scene, a hale old gentleman.

* * * *

Any institution that employs 480 people is important to any community. That's the normal roster of employes at the State School for Mental Defectives that is perched on Asylum Hill in East Newark.

It began as a Baptist school with a single building and four acres of ground. In 1873 the German Lutherans started a collegiate institute there. After three years, it was sold to private interests and in 1890 became an adjunct to what a less considerate age called the Syracuse Idiot Asylum for Girls. The school, now admitting both sexes, has been greatly expanded in recent years. Modern buildings spread over the hill which commands a noble view of the countryside. There are some 2,600 inmates.

* * * *

Other sidelights of Newark: German prisoners of war housed in the old high school on the park . . . Memories of the great blaze that swept East Newark in 1893 and of the Sherman Opera House fire of 1898 . . . the Warren murder of 17 years ago when a husband, wife and young son met mysterious death in their home which had been set afire, a crime never officially solved . . .

The old Bartle house built in West Miller Street in 1836 by James P. Bartle, pioneer merchant and boat owner, and torn down five years ago to make way for the new junior-senior high school. At its razing a legend that the tall hollow Corinthian columns housed relics of anti-Masonic days was exploded. Nothing was found in them but old newspapers. In the days of the anti-Masonic agitation, Newark's lodge met there in secret. Some members wanted to turn in the charter but 16 remained steadfast and today the lodge is one of the oldest in continuous existence in the state . . . Seeing the name Edgett on a cannery building recalled that Ezra A. Edgett in 1865 opened the pioneer cannery in the region. Eight years before at Camden he had canned the first green corn ever put up west of the Hudson. His "plant" was a row of cauldron kettles strung on poles . . . Newark also has the Comstock Cannery, second largest in the Empire State.

Another landmark is the Thomas homestead, a charming example of New England architecture, of brick with wooden wing and enclosed porch, which was built prior to 1831. Its present owner, Mrs. Martha Thomas Comstock, was born in that house which has been in her family for 90 years.

Seeing the many names beginning with Van and De, which told that the influx of Hollanders that peopled the Williamson-Marion region spilled over into Arcadia long ago . . . The name, Van Horne, on a sign recalled the blue-eyed, flaxen-haired girl from Newark who used to be University of Rochester correspondent for The Democrat and Chronicle and who went to New York and became a radio columnist. Only recently Harriet Van Horne was acclaimed as the outstanding woman columnist of the metropolis.

The eight mile Newark and Marion Railroad, one of the shortest lines still in operation in the state. It once ran passenger trains but now only operates freights "on call" to link Newark with thriving Marion, in the heart of America's greatest celery-growing region. . . .

* * * *

In 1823 when Wayne County was set apart from Ontario, "the Mother of the Counties," the Grand Canal was in process of construction.

Canandaigua, the capital of the frontier, was not on the waterway and she foresaw the rise of pushing new rivals on the route of the Canal. So when the new county was formed, crafty Canandaigua saw to it that the boundary lines were drawn so that Ontario County would have a port just within her borders. Look at a map today and note the jog that places Port Gibson in Ontario County and not in Wayne.

So Port Gibson, Canandaigua's link with the Clinton Ditch, came into being, three miles west of Newark. Canandaiguans bought the village site from the pioneer, Stephen (Squire) Allen. The port was named after a prominent Canandaiguan, Henry B. Gibson, one of the purchasers, and her streets honor men of the Finger Lakes city: Atwater, Granger, Greig, Field. And of course, there's a Canandaigua Street. For many years Port Gibson was a leading shipping point on the canal. Wagons rumbled over the hills 18 miles from Canandaigua, from Holcomb and other Ontario County communities.

Port Gibson had two malthouses, a big warehouse, two canal groceries, one on either side of the Ditch; line barns, a planing mill and barrel factory, a hotel, a creamery. Once this port was quite a town. It's mighty quiet now.

When the Barge Canal was built, considerably to the northward, it created a picturesque widewaters but left Canandaigua's port stranded on her hilltop above the old waterway. Now two-thirds of the Barge Canal there is in Ontario and the other third in Wayne County. Once it was all in Ontario. Canandaigua saw to that in 1823.

The state highway route has been changed, too. It was carried to the north, following the old Erie towpath. The road builders gouged and filled and changed the face of the landscape considerably around Port Gibson. Now the main road bypasses the old village and about all the traveler sees is the tall church spire.

Mrs. William Garlock, whose ancestors settled in the port in 1832 has a fund of village lore. She spoke of the days when her kinsmen, the Terrys, and the Stacys, the Blossoms and the Schutts owned and ran boats on the canal. Fayette Terry was the skipper of the Annie Laurie, well remembered by old timers.

Probably you've seen the name, B. T. Babbitt, on packages and on billboards. A former canal boatman, Benjamin T. Babbitt, made his first kettle of soap on a farm west of Port Gibson, just over the Wayne County line. He peddled his product around the neighborhood, then went to New York and became a Soap King.

Port Gibson calls to mind many boyhood memories for William G. Fluker, a veteran of the Spanish-American War, now a resident of Rochester. In the early 1890's he lived as a boy in the Port Gibson Hotel which burned down a few years ago. The proprietor was a widow, Elizabeth Mott, a well known character on the canal and throughout the countryside.

Fluker recalls when there were two canal basins in the town, teeming with fish. Rochester fishermen would drive down there Sundays in horses and buggies after bullheads. Veteran anglers of the locality were Crill Cobb and "Sam Hen" Salpaugh, who in their nineties still fished on, through the ice in winter. And there was Giles Brown, who fashioned custom made boots and leather pocketbooks in the shape of a sunflower 50 years ago.

* * * *

There is no finer view along the Towpath than the one I saw from Port Gibson's peaceful, sun-kissed hilltop—a panorama of rolling hills, with here and there a drumlin born of the glacial drift; shining Erie water, lined with cottages, and stretching as far as the eye could see to the eastward—toward Arcadia.

"Once Upon a Time"

THE tall man in the blue military cloak and the powdered wig reined in his horse and the little cavalcade came to a halt.

All that sunny day of 1794, Capt. Charles Williamson, agent for British interests that owned a wilderness empire, had been following the sylvan stream that flows northward from Canandaigua Lake. Now he and his men had to come to the junction with another rippling stream, the river called by the Indians Ganargua.

The bright blue eyes of the land agent glistened as they swept the landscape. Tall elms and drooping willows hung over the waters. A huddle of log cabins, reared by the first settlers five years before, bordered the place where the waters met. All about stretched the marshy meadows, the woodland with the sunlit openings, the periphery of rounded hills.

Williamson turned to Charles Cameron, his fellow Scot and his right arm in all his frontier undertakings, saying:

"This is in miniature the union of the Rivers Rhone and Saone in France and so I shall call the town I build here Lyons."

So it came about that a yet unborn village in the American wilds at the confluence of the Canandaigua Outlet and the Ganargua was given the name of an Old World city at the meeting place of two greater rivers.

* * * *

The town that Williamson laid out so long ago became a place of consequence and the commercial, political and cultural hub of a rich countryside.

In the beginning the river brought her settlers and was the principal avenue of travel. Then the Clinton Ditch came and soon the village sprawled far along the Erie water and over the steep hills.

Lyons has been the shire town since Wayne County was created in 1823 and the dome of her old Courthouse has gleamed among the trees like a beacon through the years, marking the seat of government and the political throne.

In the later years fortune has not always been kind to the old town. The industrial jackpot has eluded her. Her population, now under 4,000, once was well over 5,000. But about Lyons clings an air of consequence and distinction no parvenu town can attain. She will always have her traditions and her proud memories of the great days.

Around her quiet streets, voices seem to murmur the refrain, "once upon a time."

Once upon a time, men who moulded the destinies of the frontier lived in the pillared brick colonial houses on the hills above the town. Later on, in Lyons' commercial heydey, other powerful men built the more ornate Victorian mansions under the stately trees.

There, once upon a time, flowered an old regime, a gracious way of life, a social elegance and a cultural interest that was distinctively Lyons.

From the mansions—and from humbler homes, as well—went out boys and girls who became distinguished in many fields, captains of industry, admirals, musicians, poets, soldiers, artists among them.

The aristocratic tradition is only one facet of the Lyons personality. The pioneer strain of New England and the South has been mixed with the blood of German, Irish and Italian emigrants, to give the town warmth and color.

Lyons is like a fine old race horse, a thoroughbred, full of years and glorious memories, waiting, a little wistfully, for the Grand Circuit days to come once more.

*   *   *   *

Lyons was born at the union of the waters that Williamson later so admired.

In May of 1789 the first settlers came, 11 of them, in flat boats from Albany over the tortuous water route. They were the Stansell brothers, William and Nicholas, and their brother-in-law, John Featherly, their wives and five children.

They built a log cabin where the Outlet pours into the Ganargua to form the Clyde River, near the giant elm that became known as the Council Tree because there the settlers smoked the peace pipe with the Senecas in the nearby Indian village.

When Williamson came, there were a half dozen cabins at what the pioneers called "The Forks."

They were squatters in a sort of No Man's Land called the Gore, the strip between the first and erroneous Pre-emption Line and the second and correct one, marking the division between the lands claimd by New York and by Massachusetts. When Phelps and Gorham bought most of what is now Western New York, they caused the second survey which moved the Pre-emption Line to the east.

Then the holdings were sold to a British syndicate headed by Sir William Pultney, whose agent, the dashing Williamson, came in 1794 to claim the Gore as part of the Pultney purchase—and to found the village he christened Lyons.

Williamson made an amicable financial settlement with the colony at the Forks and then began laying out the village, with straight, wide streets centering around a public square, just as he plotted Bath, Geneva, and Sodus Point. He sold lots, built warehouses, taverns, stores along the river. He built large flour mills at Alloway, three miles south of Lyons and put Henry Towar in charge of them. In 1804 they burned. The coming of the canal sealed Alloway's fate.

In the 1830's, after Williamson was dead and Robert Troup was land agent in his stead, settlers on the Pultney lands waged a bloodless revolt against their British landlords because of usurous interest rates. They held mass meetings and prepared to resist any attempts to evict them. But with the adoption of laws mitigating the abuses and the gradual passing of lands from British hands, the trouble blew over.

*　　*　　*　　*

In 1797 Daniel Dorsey, a Maryland planter, came with 40 slaves to dwell on 1,600 acres he had purchased from Williamson. He built a mansion at the end of a long lane, lined with slave cabins, off the Geneva Turnpike and became a leader in the new community. Soon he liberated his Negroes. Slave holding was unprofitable and unpopular in the Northern clime.

The other day I visited the historic Dorsey acres. The present owner of much of the tract is James Smart, who lives on land his great-grandfather, James Dunn, bought from Dorsey nearly 120 years ago. Dunn, bound for Ohio, to take up land, stepped off a canal packet at Lyons to look around, liked the country so well that he settled there instead. In 1834 he built the three-story brick house south of the railroad tracks.

Jim Smart, who has a sentimental regard for his historic heritage, showed me where the Dorsey mansion had stood and the site of the Dorsey barn where in 1810 was held the first Genesee Conference of the Methodist Church, presided over by the famous Francis Asbury. One hundred years later, notables of Methodism came to Lyons to mark the centennial of the Conference.

Smart pointed out the pasture that he believes was the site of the old Indian village because so many arrowheads have been picked up there. He showed where only a few years ago, when a raceway that once led from the Outlet to the Dorsey mills was being filled in, a skeleton was found. It was that of a young male Negro, probably one of Judge Dorsey's Maryland slaves.

Smart's grandfather once grew tobacco on the land, in the southern tradition. There is a story that the blood of the Dorseys flows in the veins of a Maryland girl, so beloved by a British king that he gave up his throne to marry her. She, of course, is Wallis Warfield Simpson, Duchess of Windsor.

In 1812 Lyons had sixty families and was an established center in the sparsely settled frontier. The Grand Canal made it a boom town in 1822.

Men of influence such as Myron Holley, one of the fathers of the Canal, and Judge Ambrose Spencer, came to live in Lyons. Streets bear their names today. The Joppa Land Company was formed and the eastern end of village was developed. Williamson had concentrated at the western edge along the river.

The Albany Argus in 1826, describing Wayne County canal towns, said:

"Palmyra is a wealthy and popular town."

"Arcadia is a wealthy and respectable town."

But about Lyons it waxed more eloquent: "Lyons is densely populated. It is built on handsome dry ground rising to gentle acclivity to the west and north from the canal and is flanked by a romantic ridge."

The canal pumped commercial lifeblood into Lyons. The first ditch ran through the heart of the village. Canal Street marks its path. The enlargement of the waterway changed the route and Erie water sloshed against the backs of the stores in William Street.

But the Barge Canal utilized the Clyde River, considerably to the southward, and left gaping holes in the village, where the older ditch had run, marring the regular pattern of streets the founding fathers had mapped so carefully.

*   *   *   *

Lyons' industrial record is an imposing one but again that "Once upon a time" refrain intrudes.

For many years she was a world center of the peppermint and essential oil business and H. G. Hotchkiss of Lyons was the "peppermint king." As early as 1830, farmers were growing mint in the region. In 1841 Hotchkiss began putting up the oils in the gray building that still stands in Water Street.

The industry grew until in 1868, nearly 300 acres were under cultivation, and nearly every farmer in the area was growing mint for Hotchkiss. The product was shipped all over the globe, notably to England. The Lyons plants in 1877 were the largest of their kind in the world. But like so many other Lyons industries, this one had to bow to new trends, although today another H. G. Hotchkiss, the third of his line, is still shipping essential oils from the same old depot. But the mint beds no longer dot the hills and vales of Wayne.

Once upon a time there were potteries along the old canal which brought in the clay and carried away the finished products, jugs of exquisite workmanship among them. The red brick buildings that once housed the industry are now apartments.

Lyons had an important silver plate industry, at its zenith in the 1890's. Up to about 1910 she had the largest sugar beet refinery

Dynamic Newark, Pierced by "The Ditch"

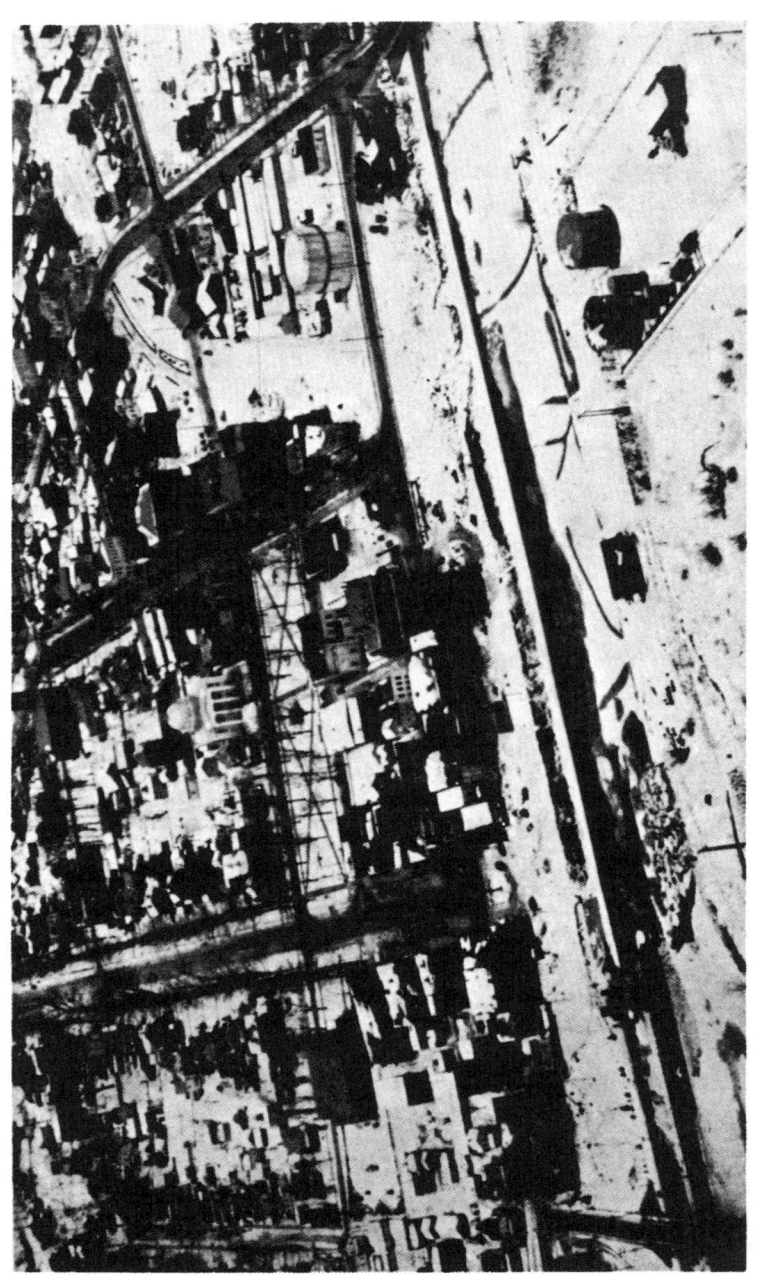

Stately Lyons, "Hub of Wayne"

in the East. She had big malthouses, glove factories, tanneries, brickyards, besides foundries in "Dutchtown" on the east side.

Among the shire town's oldtime industries was the Deuchler carriage shop which flourished for two generations and died with the advent of the motor vehicle. The shop made top notch carriages and sleighs and for many years had the contract for heavy bobs for Standard Oil. Everything was hand made.

Lyons today has a dehydrating plant, an apple brandy distillery, a fruit packing plant, a powdered egg industry. She is in the heart of the rich Wayne County fruit and vegetable belt and from the beginning has been a produce shipping center.

The great Newark nursery industry is not confined to the town of Arcadia. The Jackson-Perkins Company, on a large tract called Perkinsville southeast of Lyons, has a bed of 100,000 roses and an orchard of nearly half a million young peach trees.

Thousands have known Lyons as a railroad transfer point, with three lines of the New York Central converging there. Once upon a time, the big car shops of the Central gave employment to 200 to 250 men. When the shops pulled up stakes in 1923, it was a sad day for Lyons.

* * * *

In 1874 a son was born to William Taylor, a prosperous Lyons tanner of pioneer stock. He was named Myron Charles but everybody in the village called him Charley. He went to the village school, got good marks, was not particularly athletic, played the guitar and sang in the Presbyterian choir. He was a good mixer and everyone liked him.

After graduating from Cornell, he came back home to practice law. Oldtimers remember times when business was slack in the law office, Charley would help haul tan bark to his father's tannery. He was a gregarious chap who would quaff an occasional glass of cider with a farmer client.

Taylor's father engaged in the manufacture of mail pouches and Uncle Sam was his leading customer. Myron went out on the road to buy materials, and formed contacts with important financial figures. He went to New York and became a titan of industry, the steelmaster who electrified the business world by making peace with John L. Lewis when other magnates were for battle to the death with the miners' chieftain. As everybody knows, the late President Roosevelt made Lyons-born Myron Charles Taylor his personal envoy to the Vatican.

This millionaire has not forgotten his home town. He gave the site of the old Taylor tannery to the village for a park. The dignified gray brick house with green blinds in the heart of town is now a community center through his generosity and children romp on the lawns and in the old stables. He has given liberally to churches and to other local causes, often insisting that the benefactions be kept secret.

* * * *

There are other glittering names on the roster of native sons and daughters: William M. Stewart, promoter of the fabulous Comstock Lode and once senator from Nevada; Admiral Bradley A. Fiske, who fought with Dewey at Manila Bay and invented many electrical devices for use on warships; another admiral, Willard Bronson, at one time head of the United States Naval Academy.

There were the artists: De Witt Parshall, painter of Western scenes; Birgetta Moran Farmer, Claire Sherwood, Emma Rudd and Sarah Veeder among them.

A Lyons girl today is winning fame in an unusual field—the painting of race horses. She is Ann Collins, who has numbered among her clients, Col. E. R. Bradley, Bing Crosby and other turf notables. Her painting of Baron Jack hangs in New York's Club 21. As this is written, Miss Collins is back home, completing a painting of Bobinet. Race track followers will recognize the name.

In the field of music there was William Sherwood, pupil of the great pianist Liszt. He was the son of the Rev. Lyman Sherwood whose Lyons Music Academy in its day made the shire town such an artistic center. Pupils came from as far distant as Florida.

And there was Frank (Fay) Darling, for 15 years musical director for Flo Ziegfeld. At 9 he was playing a church organ in Lyons; at 18 he was a musical director in New York. On retirement he came back to live in Lyons where he died in 1935. His widow lives near the big high school and her home is filled with autographed pictures and other mementoes of the stars with whom her husband was associated: Anna Held, who was his pupil; Will Rogers, whom he knew in the Follies; Raymond Hitchcock, Bert Williams and many more.

* * * *

Mary Ashley Van Voorhis Townsend spent most of her mature life in New Orleans but she was born in a farm house west of Lyons of old Dutch stock. After she had attained considerable renown as a poetess in the South, her thoughts kept straying back to the scenes of her girlhood. So in 1877 there appeared in the New York Post a nostalgic poem which began:

> "Ye hills of Wayne! ye hills of Wayne!
> In dreams I see your slopes again;
> In dreams my childish feet explore
> Your daisied dells, beloved of yore:
> In dreams, with eager feet I press
> Far up your heights of loveliness,
> And stand, a glad-eyed girl again,
> Upon the happy hills of Wayne."

* * * *

For decades bald, mustached Charles H. Betts of Lyons was boss of Wayne County and a power in the state councils of the Grand Old Party. The publisher of the Lyons Republican (founded in 1821) was a stalwart of the Old Guard, lining up with Barnes of Albany, the Wadsworths of Geneseo and Aldridge of Rochester in their battles against Teddy Roosevelt and Charles E. Hughes.

George K. Shuler, World War I hero, Democratic state treasurer in 1922–24, was another Lyons native. He came out of the war, a captain of Marines, his breast covered with decorations for gallantry in action. He is the same handsome captain of Marines who figured, through no fault of his own, in the Teapot Dome tempest of the Harding era. Acting under orders, he led a company of Marines to a Wyoming oil field to dispossess the occupants so that the property might pass to a great oil company involved in the conspiracy.

* * * *

The old canal figured in the political picture, especially in the spring, when the ditch was due for its annual cleaning. The purging lasted two or three weeks and involved considerable patronage, valuable to the party in power. A ramp of saw horses and planks led from the Towpath to the canal bottom. As one veteran observer put it: "Coming at village election time, the cleaning of the canal bed also helped clean the opposition political party. Shovels were distributed instead of dollars."

* * * *

There are so many memories of old Lyons and the old Canal, so many landmarks.

There is the Glover house, built by Williamson as a storehouse along the river in 1796. It now stands in Jackson Street, a private residence with a marker on its front. It was Lyons' first meeting house; housed the first school and the first court.

Perched on a steep hill among the old colonial houses is a dignified yellow building that would pass for another mansion. It's the Wayne County Jail.

There are memories of Lyon's cultural heyday, when there were delightful musicales in the old houses on the "romantic ridge"; when Joe Jefferson and De Wolff Hopper and other stars played in the Parshall Memorial Opera House and special trains ran from Geneva.

Around a brick house at 100 Broad Street linger memories of a tall man in a stove pipe hat who spent a night here in 1863 after a torchlight parade through the streets of Lyons. The guest was Abraham Lincoln and his host was Maj. Alexander B. Williams, then paymaster of the Union Army.

There are sad memories of Lyons' greatest catastrophe, the fire which destroyed the high school in 1920 and cost the lives of two young girl pupils. It was two days before Christmas and they were trapped on the third floor where they had been decorating a stage.

And there are pleasant memories in gray heads of winter nights when the band played and the lights were bright and boys and girls skated on the frozen Erie water at ice festivals of long ago.

*   *   *   *

For former Police Judge Edward D. Bourne, a fine figure of a man at 80, there are memories of his boyhood when he hitched rides on log rafts going through town; of the old double locks at the foot of Broad Street; when there were three Lyons-owned boats on the Ditch and the docks were piled with goods and produce.

He repeated a tale he had heard from his father: How 110 years ago the elder Bourne had seen a packet boat of German settlers, bound for Ohio, halted at Lyons; how they visited the hotel operated at Montezuma and Church Streets by Philip Dorsheimer and were so impressed by the innkeeper's "sales talk" in their native tongue that they left the packet, set up their kettles on a tripod in the park and stayed in Lyons, to found families well known in the village.

Miss Anna Avery, who was born on a farm along the Ditch and who has delved deeply into early canal history, remembers her father telling her about seeing the lighted packets gliding by in the night. She told of Pilgrimport, a Holy Rollerish colony that pitched its tents along the waterway during the rise of the "Isms."

Lyons' halcyon sporting days were recalled by William R. Courneen, veteran newspaper correspondent. Once Lyons had a team in the old State League; such stars at Pat Moran and Billy Gilbert wore Lyons uniforms and Mike Sweeney, the Rochester contractor, managed the home team. The diamond was on the old County Fair grounds, now bisected by the Barge Canal.

From his window in the County Clerk's office where he has served for more than 30 years, Charles A. Noble looked across the shady park to the old court-house with the massive pillars, where so much Wayne County history has been written, and talked of other days. Noble has lived all his 77 years in Lyons. He once was joint owner of a hardware store along the old canal at the foot of Broad Street, and has many recollections of colorful towpath days.

Noble's political mentor was Charles Betts and on the publisher's death he took the mantle of Republican leadership. Only recently he turned over the county chairmanship to Mrs. Mildred Taylor, the first woman in the state to hold the office.

Noble glanced across the park to the Court House, his kindly blue eyes alight with memories, and said: "There have been some famous trials there—the Kelly gang that murdered the Sodus night watchman and Oliver Curtis Perry. . . ."

* * * *

Oliver Curtis Perry—the name conjures up an incongruous picture of a soft spoken, mild mannered youth, dressed in sober black, who on Feb. 22, 1892, wrote into Western New York's criminal history its most bizarre chapter. He was the "man who stole a train."

Perry, then only 27 but with a price on his head for train robbery, secreted himself on a ten car all-express train as it left Syracuse. In the money car was the prize he sought, nearly a quarter of a million dollars, guarded by a lone messenger, Daniel T. McInerney of Rochester.

At Jordan he entered the money car after lowering himself from the roof by means of an ingenious rope ladder with hooks that fitted over its side, and smashed the window with the butt of one of his two revolvers. There ensued a fierce gun duel. The messenger, thrice wounded, crumpled to the floor, but before he lost consciousness, he gave a feeble pull at the bell cord, plunged the car into blackness by kicking over the lamp and sat on the money packages.

Perry was thwarted. The conductor, Emil Laas of Rochester, heard the pull at the cord and raced back to the money car, only to look into the bandit's guns. At Port Byron, Laas succeeded in stopping the train. The crew found the wounded messenger, the treasure intact but no bandit. They concluded Perry had slunk off the train.

At Lyons he was spotted in the gathering crowd and as railroad men made for him, the bandit commandeered a standing freight engine and opening the throttle wide, headed east. Perry knew how to run a locomotive for he had worked in railroad shops before he took up banditry. The railroaders, armed with a shotgun, gave pursuit on a parallel track in the express engine.

It was a fantastic chase. When the bandit saw the pursuing engine, he reversed, raking the other cab with bullets as it flashed by. When the express engine reversed, Perry went forward, to the accompaniment of gunfire. This procedure was repeated until finally the railroaders gave up the chase.

Perry abandoned his locomotive at the "Blue Cut" west of Lyons, and fled across fields. In his flight he commandeered, first a farmer's horse which he rode, and later a horse and cutter. He got on a dead end road and crouched behind a stone fence to await developments.

There a sheriff's posse, led by the late colorful Jerry Collins, then a deputy, found him and captured him through a ruse.

While he was in the Lyons jail, awaiting trial, the two-gun desperado hatched two vain escape plots. His trial packed the Courthouse and wound up with this sentence:

"Forty-nine years and three months in state's prison."

Perry spent 39 bizarre years behind the bars. He blinded himself in his cell, he went on hunger strikes, he refused to wear prison garb, he wrote appeals to the governor, asking a pardon.

Before he died in Dannemora's madhouse, Oliver Curtis Perry boasted:

"Nobody ever stole a train just the way I did."

I reckon nobody ever did.

*". . . a roamin' in the gloamin'
On the bonnie bank of Clyde."*

Bonnie Banks

IT was years ago that I heard Harry Lauder sing the old song but I can close my eyes and see the litle gray minstrel in his plaids and kilties, prancing out on the stage of Rochester's old Lyceum, and hear again the delightful Scotch burr rolling out the refrain like the skirl of bagpipes in "the Heelands."

And now in 1945, I was roaming the bonnie banks of the York State Clyde and it was "in the gloaming," the twilight of my Towpath jaunt.

For in the braw old town of Clyde my "Canal Zone" ends.

*   *   *   *

Clyde's background is heterogeneous.

Named by a Scot, she was settled by Yankees, her streets were laid out by a one-time commander of Hessian mercenaries and today her citizens of Italian origin outnumber any other foreign stock.

Her roots go deeper back into recorded history than any other canal town in the area. In 1722 when New York was a province of the British crown, the site of Clyde was a fortified outpost guarding the route of the British fur trade. In the beginning her name was Blockhouse.

Clyde is in the Military Tract which was set aside for veterans of the Revolutionary War. She is the first canal town east of the Pre-emption Line. At her eastern border stretches the great Montezuma swamp, the miry monster before whom all the canal diggers quailed, all save the men from the bogs of Erin. The pioneers shunned the swamp as worthless but a later generation has transformed it into rich mucklands.

Clyde (Population 2,356), is not a spectacular town, not given much to pomp. She is, however, a substantial and a busy one and through the years has sailed along on a pretty even keel. She has a harmonious racial blend of Yankee, Dutch, Irish and Italian stocks. In rock-ribbed Republican Wayne County, she is the town most likely to kick over the GOP apple cart.

When the "Direct Line," the Rochester & Syracuse Railroad, was built over 90 years ago, the route was so direct that it skirted the villages of Macedon, Palmyra, Newark and Lyons. But it ran directly into the heart of Clyde. So did the late lamented Rochester, Syracuse & Eastern trolley line. Today the Main Line of the Central, the West Shore and the Clyde River, now a part of the Barge Canal, run side by side under a great bridge near the center of the village.

Practical minded Clyde has her traditions. She has had her dreams of glory. Once she hoped the mineral spring in her park would make her a famous spa. A persistent vision, born in the 1830's and revived in the 20th Century, was that of a canal linking Great Sodus Bay with the Erie Canal at Clyde.

Over the broad river valley, the drumlins keep eternal brooding vigil. Some of the hill formations might well have been shaped by a fanciful child playing with wet earth. Some are as fantastic as a cubist sketch. Others are merely rounded hills rising at irregular intervals from the plain.

No gallery houses a more striking picture than the one I saw near Clyde, a big, black farm horse, silhouetted on the apex of a pear-shaped drumlin, against a flaming sunset.

* * * *

About Clyde's early name of Blockhouse hangs many a colorful tale.

In 1722, William Burnet, provincial governor of New York, seeking to clinch the frontier fur trade for the crown, sent a small detachment under Capt. Peter Schuyler, Jr., to protect the Great Lakes routes by building trading posts and forts. At the site of Clyde a blockhouse was built, commanding the river and guarding the trail to Lake Ontario.

It soon was abandoned. Its later career was a checkered one. Nomadic bands of whites and Indians used it during the French and Indian wars. After the Revolution, it was a base for marauding British Redcoats and smugglers. It became such a nuisance that in 1800 the government sent troops to burn it down.

So when the first permanent settlers came to the locality, they found only the charred ruins of the old blockhouse. But the name stuck to the site for years.

In 1820 a rumor spread that a large sum of money had been hidden near the historic spot and moonlight nights saw much feverish digging for buried treasure—that never was uncovered.

The Clyde region from time immemorial was a mecca for hunters and trappers but there was no permanent settlement in the town until 1800 when Laomi Beedle came to Marengo, three miles south of the present Clyde. The next year two boatloads of Kings, Gregorys and Millses settled in the same locality.

By 1810 there were a half dozen families living on the south bank of the river and the place was called Lauraville in honor of Henrietta Laura, Countess of Bath, the daughter of Sir William Pultney, head of the great British land syndicate.

Two years later the township of Galen was formed. It was named after the Greek physician and this part of the Military Tract was intended for surgeons of the Revolution. But there is no record of any influx of army medicos into Galen Town.

In 1815 the "Father of Clyde" entered the picture in the person of Maj. Frederick Augustus De Zeng, son of a baron of Saxony. He came to America at the head of a company of Hessians in the Revolution. Stationed in New York, he never was called upon to fight the colonists. Infatuated with the new country, he foreswore his Old World title and allegiance and became a citizen of the United States.

After promoting the pioneer canal project at Little Falls where he also founded glass works, De Zeng bought a tract from the Pultney interests on the north side of the river then known as the Ganargua or Mud Creek. He started laying out a village site. His son, William S., completed the work and established the glass factory that for nearly a century was an important Clyde industry.

In 1818 Andrew McNab began selling village lots on the north bank of the river which, because he fancied it resembled another stream he had known as a boy in his native Scotland, he renamed the Clyde. He called the village by the same name and to carry out the Scottish motif, christened the principal thoroughfare Glasgow Street, a name it bears today.

About that time there was considerable excitement at Lauraville across the river over the discovery of a salt spring. Its operation did not prove profitable.

*   *   *   *

Then in 1822 the Grand Canal was dug through the valley of the Clyde and it was the old familiar story. The tiny settlement sprang into vigorous life. That year the Griswolds, Aaron and Simeon, launched the Gold Hunter, the first Clyde-owned canal boat.

Lock Berlin, in the maple forest to the west, became a canal port, and in the early days, it was a wild and wooly one. The hamlet is peaceful enough today. In utilizing the river, the Barge Canal by-passed Lock Berlin. The Clinton Ditch ended the supremacy of Marengo on the Genesee Turnpike, the stage coach route, and it lapsed into somnolence.

Taverns clustered around the packet dock and the locks at Clyde, among them one with the picturesque name of the Indian Queen. Logging flourished on the river and when the Clyde went on spring rampages, the logs sometimes floated right into the business district.

In 1835 Lauraville was merged with Clyde and the village was incorporated in W. S. Stow's little law office which today is a part of the gasoline station at the head of the village park.

This park, which contains the famous mineral spring, was at first a common where cattle grazed. When in the 1856's, a high board fence was put around it and cattle fairs were held there, the villagers, deprived of their free pasturage, raised such a rumpus that the fence came down in a short time.

* * * *

Clyde has always been an industrial and trading center. It had iron works as early as 1820. In 1850 the father of Charles T. Saxton, one of the village's most distinguished sons and a onetime lieutenant governor of New York, was making coach lace. J. M. Jones, who later made printing presses at Palmyra, in 1852 was manufacturing a crude pioneer typewriter at Clyde.

Once the village had nine malt-houses. The glass works, which lasted until 1912, was the birthplace of the Mason type of fruit jar. At the turn of the century, glass blowers were receiving $8 a day, an unheard of wage in those times.

Clyde's industry today is centered around a large cannery and the Acme plant which had important contracts for electrical apparatus during the war and which recently became part of the big General Electric system. The industrial skies are bright over the bonnie banks.

* * * *

In St. John's Episcopal Church is a pipe organ that goes back to the reign of Queen Anne. Said to have been the first of its kind in the state, it once belonged to historic Trinity Church in New York and from there found its way, first to Trinity Church in Geneva, and, a century ago, to Clyde.

In 1836 a village ordinance was adopted providing that "any person or persons who shall hereafter suffer or permit any playing with cards or dice or any gaming table or shuffleboard or shall permit any gaming by lot or chance within his or her house, outhouse, yard or garden within the Village of Clyde, shall for every offense forfeit or pay into the village treasury the sum of $10." I was told the law has never been formally repealed.

Incidentally, Clyde is one of the sportiest towns on the Towpath.

* * * *

The Irish came with the Clinton Ditch and the first railroad. The building of the West Shore more than half a century ago brought the Italians. About the only one of the original Italian settlers still living is the venerable Santo Salerno. A monument in the village park, erected by the Sons of Italy to the memory of George Washington, attests to the community spirit of this racial group.

Clyde is not without her Old Family traditions. In other days there were the Saxtons, politically potent; the Elys who ran the glass works and lived in the pillared mansion in West Genesee Street, now a noble ruin; the Briggses who ran the bank—and many others.

And there were the Vandenbergs, among them John, the lawyer, and Aaron, who operated a harness shop. The Aaron Vandenbergs moved to Michigan some 70 years ago and there a son was born to them who was named Arthur H. This son went to work on a Grand Rapids newspaper as a reporter. In a few years he owned the paper. Then he went to the United States Senate where he became the most authoritative voice on the Republican side. This year he was appointed by the late President Roosevelt as a member of the United States delegation to the San Francisco World Security Conference.

Some old timers in Clyde thought that Senator Vandenberg had lived in the village as a boy; others were sure he never did. To clear the matter up, I wrote to the Senator and received a prompt and informative answer. He wrote:

"I was not born in Clyde although both my father and mother came from Clyde. I was born in Grand Rapids, Mich., after my parents had moved west about 1875. My mother belonged to one of the most distinguished old Clyde families. She was the daughter of Dr. Aaron T. Hendrick. . . . My father ran a harness shop in Clyde. I believe he was deputy postmaster under President Grant. One of my uncles was Samuel H. Briggs of the Briggs Bank at Clyde. As a small child I returned with my mother to Clyde on several occasions; but I am sorry to say it has not been possible for me to get back to the old town for many long years."

Arthur Hendrick Vandenberg, one of the most influential figures of contemporary politics, has not forgotten the old town in York State that he knew as a child and where his father once ran a harness shop and sold buggy whips.

* * * *

Barney Willson is a walking encyclopedia of Clyde lore. He was christened Bion but everybody calls him Barney. He's in his 88th year but spry as a grasshopper. Summers he works his garden back of his rickety old house on the south bank of the river. Popcorn is his chief crop and for years he has sold it in the village. Winters he does some trapping. Barney's wiry and witty and does not attribute his longevity to total abstinence.

Here are some of Barney's memory gems:

"In 1880 when I was 22, I drove two green horses hauling the lumber scow John McKeown from Clyde to Troy. I was 40 days on the Towpath for which I got $1 a day. I had $16 when I started. When I left, after I had collected my pay, I had $1. I was green as my horses, a sucker for them old canallers. Besides, one of the horses tugged so hard I wore the soles off my shoes and the other one nearly fell into the ditch. No more Towpath for me after that.

"I remember when there were wood-burning engines on the railroad through Clyde; when the tracks crossed at grade and there was only a little swing bridge across the river; when I worked at the mason's trade for 25 cents a day and butter was 11 cents a pound; pork $3 per hundred pounds; eggs 6 cents a dozen and whisky 25 cents a gallon. When I worked in harvest, they used to serve corn liquor to us by the dipperful every three hours."

Barney remembers when the now towering elms and maples were set out in the village park, then enclosed by a low rail fence; when the mineral water from the spring there was bottled by Lawyer Baker and shipped from Clyde; and, in the days before the use of coal, when the men in the glass factory would go out into the woods and cut huge logs for fires to melt the glass.

Barney's father, Henry P. Willson, helped put the logs in the old corduroy road. "They're still there under Glasgow Street," remarked Barney as he scampered off across the long bridge to tend his popcorn patch.

* * * *

The Towpath on Bonnie Banks of Clyde

De Witt Clinton at "The Marriage of the Waters"

Before the Barge Canal came, the Erie ditch ran through the heart of the village and it is easy to trace the old route back of the stores, south of the present waterway. There were memories of old Towpath days when Canal Street was lined with grog shops; when Bill (Muley) McDougall of Clyde, "as broad as he was tall," could lick anybody on the canal; when youngsters, now Clyde business men, used to hurl ribald rhymes and an occasional stone at "the hoggies!"

In Lyons I called on Miss Ella Fee, a retired school teacher, who spent her early years on her father's farm along the Erie water at the now extinct port of Lockpit, also called Meadville, east of Clyde.

From her I first heard of the "bum boats." They were rowboats in which farmers would go out, with fresh vegetables and fruit, to meet the canal boats, hitching to their sides and passing up the produce to the canallers as they crept along. Then the "bum boats" would hitch a ride back home, hence the name.

Miss Fee, who as a girl occasionally accompanied her brothers on these "bum boat" expeditions, recalled how eager the canal wives were to get fresh produce and what "happy people the canal folk were, forever singing to the accompaniment of violin or accordion."

She called to mind winters when sleighs traveled to and from town on the frozen canal and how, when the water was let out of the ditch, men and boys in hip boots would take bushels of bullheads out of the soft mud. The fish went down into the mud instead of going out with the water.

*   *   *   *

And here beside the bonnie banks of the Clyde, I must say farewell to the Towpath. I was loath to quit the trail of memories where phantom voices still sang out across the years:

"Low bridge, everybody down."

My Towpath ramble had begun with a tugboat ride to the Orleans blossom country when all the land was green with spring. It was ending in the hills of Wayne with the smoky tang of autumn in the air.

It began amid a world at war. Since, victory and peace—and the atomic bomb—had come to streak across the world horizon the dazzling dawn of a portentous new day.

But calmly the Erie water rolls on, across the state it had made great, through the busy towns it had mothered—unheeding the clash of changing moods.

It, too, in its time had shaped the course of history.

THE END

Arch Merrill's New York

Twenty-three volumes comprise the series of regional history and folklore created by Arch Merrill from the 1940s through the 1960s.

Watch for additional volumes of the series at your favorite bookstore or send a postal card and request to be placed on our mailing list for notification as future titles are released.

Empire State Books
a division of
Heart of the Lakes Publishing
PO Box 299
Interlaken, NY 14847

Arch Merrill's New York

Mary Jemison, captured as a young girl of 15 in colonial Pennsylvania and adopted by the Senecas. After marriage her Indian family migrated to the area of the Genesee flats below the falls in the area that is now Letchworth State Park. She received title to the land at the Treaty of Big Tree and the family lived there for many years.

Nun-da-wag-ga was a natural paradise; white men wished to possess it having once seen it. The land was wrested from the Senecas in 1797. Still prized today, the hills and valleys are thought to be the most beautiful in upstate New York. Merrill's tales again bring to life the long history of the area.

Empire State Books
Interlaken, NY 14847

Arch Merrill's New York

Ten long, slender strips of blue in the middle of the New York State map. Lakes, cities, villages—all have personalities of their own which are brought to life in the writings of western New York's folk historian, Arch Merrill. The Lake Guns of Seneca, Copper John of Auburn, the Curse of Keuka, and the tales of the cities all brought back to life in this most popular of Merrill's books.

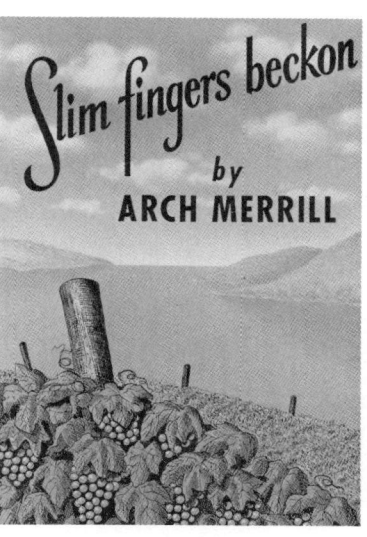

Considered the rarest of the Merrill books, many of the stories included are now *Shadows on the Wall* but in their own time they were the news items that caught the interest of the region. The seven Sutherland sisters with the longest hair in the world; Rulloff, the scholarly "Fiend of the Finger Lakes;" and the world's first jinrikisha built in a wagon shop above Keuka Lake.

Empire State Books
Interlaken, NY 14847

Arch Merrill's New York

The Flour City has a long history from its birth as a crossroad milling village to become the milling center of America's breadbasket, the Genesee Valley. It later became the Flower City, the nursery capital of America in the latter part of the 1800s. Today it is known as the photographic capital of the nation. Rochester has led an interesting life and stories abound of individuals and institutions. The reader will delve back into the past to find Rattlesnake Pete, Susan B. Anthony, Frederick Douglass, and Frogleg George. The Driving Park, the Glen House, the Arcade, the Liberty Pole, the Eastman Theater—landmarks of the past and present are found in this volume about Merrill's adopted home, Rochester.

Empire State Books
Interlaken, NY 14847

Also Available

J. Sheldon Fisher has collected oral history since his childhood; now in his 80s, his recall of them is as clear as the day he first heard them. *The Groaning Tree* is his first published collection of some of these stories. Menzo's prize rooster, snowbound, the happy well digger and Henry Garling's mad cow will and other stories will add humor to your day.

In 1840, young Marco and his mentor set out for adventure in the pursuit of knowledge of the operation of canals. Starting at Albany to study the operation of the Erie Canal, they ride on a packet boat to Schoharie, describing the scenes along the way as well as the events on the packet boat. A book for young readers, first published in 1843.

Empire State Books
Interlaken, NY 14847

Also Available

Rochester journalist Lloyd E. Klos has brought together many of his weekly nostaliga columns into three volumes of *A Resident's Recollections*. Trollies, theaters, big bands, old cars, famous personalities, and the little things of life are among the memories that are brought back to life.

The *Rochester and Eastern Rapid Railway* was an interurban that connected Rochester to Geneva and Seneca Lake. Known as the "Orange Limited" it was proclaimed the fastest on rails after beating a steam engine in a race near Victor in Ontario County. This history from Rochester rail buff and author, William Reed Gordon.

Empire State Books
Interlaken, NY 14847